بسم الله الرحمن الرحيم

لا إله إلا الله

DAWAH
THE LOST ART OF THE CALL OF ISLAM

DAWAH

THE LOST ART OF THE CALL OF ISLAM

A Physical, Spiritual, & Social Healing

SHEIKH KHALID AMIN

DETROIT, MI

Dawah: The Lost Art of the Call of Islam.
A Physical, Spiritual, and Social Healing

Copyright © 2021 by Sheikh Khalid Amin

Published in the United States by Book Power Publishing, an imprint of Niyah Press, Detroit, Michigan.
www.bookpowerpublishing.com

No part of this book may be used or reproduced in any manner whatsoever without written permission except in the case of brief quotations.

Book Power Publishing books may be purchased for educational, business, or sales promotional use. For study groups, email us at *info@bookpowerpublishing.com*

Contact the author at: ambassadorsofhumanity@gmail.com

Cover Designer: www.nurdesignco.com

First Edition

PRINTED IN THE UNITED STATES OF AMERICA.

ISBN: 978-1-945873-41-6

CONTENTS

Glossary Xv
Witnesses' Statements Xvii
Fautimah Amin's Testimonial Regarding
Her Husband, Khalid Amin:................................. Xxii

Chapter 1   Important Dawah Advice 1
                1.1 Excellence In The Invitation To Heal.......... 1
                1.2 Dawah, The Lost Art 4
                1.3 Why Is It So Important To Be An Inviter To
                The Lord Of All The Worlds? 4

Chapter 2   Soul Food 7
                2.1 Remember Allah Is The
                Ultimate Reality 7
                2.2 Stay In Consultation 10
                2.3 Remember That Allah
                Controls Everything 11
                2.4 What Seems To Be Far Is Near 14
                2.5 Are We Really Ready To Be Tested? 14
                2.6 Feed The Poor 20
                2.7 Pray At Night While Others
                Are Sleeping 21
                2.8 Be Watchful 22

Chapter 3	Introduction To Being A Da'ee 23	
	Lessons For The Prospective	
	Da'ee Self-Reflection 24	
	3.1 Faith 24	
	A. Actions Of The Heart 24	
	B. Actions Of The Tongue 24	
	C. Actions Of The Body 25	
	3.2 Humility 25	
	3.3 Honesty 26	
	3.4 Truthfulness 27	
	3.5 Kindheartedness 27	
	3.6 Consideration 28	
	3.7 Share Your Time 28	
	3.8 Patience 28	
	3.9 Selflessness 28	
	3.10 Choose Your Friends, Do	
	Not Let Your Friends Choose You 29	
	3.11 Dignity 30	
Chapter 4	Training In The Field 33	
	4.1 Capture Someone's Attention	
	With A Kind Introduction 34	
	4.2 Presentation 34	
	4.3 Close On A Positive Note 35	
Chapter 5	The Social Work 37	
	5.1 Spiritually Connect People	
	With Their Lord 37	
	5.2 Taleem (Teachings) Daily In The Field ... 38	
	5.3 When Should You Have Ta'leems 39	
	5.4 Smile 39	
	5.5 The Inner Smile 39	
	5.6 Be Sensitive 39	

	5.7 Relax Others 40
	5.8 Listen With Your Heart 40
	5.9 While Someone Else Is Speaking, Make Dua For Them Silently 41
Chapter 6	Wisdoms 43
	6.1 Keep An Open Heart And Mind 43
	6.2 Knowledge 45
	6.3 Action Based On Knowledge 45
	6.4 Reach Out And Help Someone 46
	6.5 Talk To People On The Level They Are On 46
	6.6 Keep Yourself In The Spirit Of A Student 46
	6.7 Think Five Times Before You Say Something And You Might Be Right 47
	6.8 Meditate On Allah's Words And Ponder Over The Creation 49
	6.9 Sit With Others And Enjoy Silence 49
	6.10 Be Spiritually Conscious At All Times ... 50
Chapter 7	Advice To Da'ees... 53
	7.1 Be Natural 53
	7.2 Find Out What Interests A Person And Enter That Door 54
	7.3 Respect Everyone, Even The Bum 55
	7.4 Learn To Flow 55
	7.5 A Spiritual Operation 56
	7.6 Recognize Good Qualities In Others 56
	7.7 Remember The Book Of Allah Is Our Guidance 57
	7.8 Live The Sunnah (What The Prophet Did, Said, And Established), Don't Talk It 59

7.9 Pray For The Sick 60
7.10 Start When Others Stop 61
7.11 Always Be In Motion Even
If You Are Standing Still 62
7.12 Be Lively 63
7.13 Children Love Attention,
And So Do Adults 63
7.14 Be Light On Others Not Heavy 63
7.15 Be Servants 64
7.16 Be Peacemakers 65
7.17 Avoid Hellraisers 66
7.18 Be Concerned About Others 67
7.19 Visit The Sick 68
7.20 Visit The Graves 69
7.21 Make Tawheed Foremost
And Alive In Our Daily Lives 70
7.22 Reflect On One Verse At A Time 71

Chapter 8   More Advice To Da'ees 73
8.1 Always Be Willing To Share 73
8.2 Remember, Steel Is Put In
Fire To Make It Strong 74
8.3 Always Remember Allah In All
Circumstances And Conditions 74
8.4 Remember, What Seems To
Be Far Is Near 75
8.5 Follow Your First Mind 76
8.6 Don't Use Others, Help Them 76
8.7 Don't Be So Critical 77
8.8 Be Thankful If You Are Well 77
8.9 Let People In Your Front Door, Don't
Let Them Enter Through The Back Door 78
8.10 Spiritually Clean Your Own House 79

	8.11 Understand The Apparent So We Can Learn The Implied 80
	8.12 We Should Look To Be Trained, Not Look For Fame 81
	8.13 Fight Your Own Nafs 83
	8.14 Let Allah Mold You 83
Chapter 9	Real Stories From The Field 85
	9.1 A Physical Touch Can Be A Deep Spiritual Touch 85
	9.2 Get Out Of The Way And Let The Hearts Talk To One Another 85
	9.3 Reach Inward—Study Your Own History And Try To Get To Know Yourself 86
	9.4 Recognize The Spirit That We Are Dealing With 86
	9.5 Tie Your Affairs To Salah 87
	9.6 Practice Timing—Time Management 89
	9.7 Remember: Light Has Many Different Degrees And Stages 91
	9.8 Let Allah Wash Our Hearts; We Can't Do It 94
	9.9 Be Balanced 95
	9.10 Look And Listen For Keys Sent To Us By Strangers 98

Chapter 10 Landmarks, Establishing Your Own Environment 101

    10.1 Marketplaces 101
    10.2 Downtown Areas 102
    10.3 Table Dawah Downtown 104
    10.4 Universities 105

        10.5 Courthouses 106
        10.6 Government Buildings 106
        10.7 Welfare Centers 106
        10.8 Check Cashing Places 106
        10.9 Supermarkets 107
        10.10 Motor Vehicles Department 107
        10.11 Recreational Parks 108
        10.12 Festivals 108
        10.13 Door To Door 109
        10.14 Social Programs 110
        10.15 Television Programs 111
        10.16 Prisons 111
        10.17 Drug Abuse Programs 111
        10.18 Juvenile Detention Centers 111
        10.19 Detox Centers 112
        10.20 Hospital Cafeterias 112
        10.21 Outside Of Factories 112
        10.22 Tourists Places 112
        10.23 Bus Stations 113
        10.24 Amtrak Train Stations 113
        10.25 Flea Markets 113

Chapter 11 Questions And Answers 115
        Questions & Answers: 115

Chapter 12 About The Author 121
        About The Author 121
        Sheikh Khalid Amin—Translator 122

I dedicate this book to my beloved family, my loving parents George and Alma Carter, my wife Mrs. Fautimah Amin, my sons Harun, AbuBakr, and Abdullah Amin. Also to all those beautiful people who helped to develop and train us in the field of dawah for the last 52 years. It has been a long struggle filled with many trials and sacrifices. May Allah have mercy on all those unknown dedicated brothers who preceded us, many of them worked together with us in the field of dawah, but they have returned to Allah, Glorified is He.

I bear witness that there is no god but Allah and Prophet Muhammad, son of Abdullah is His last Messenger ﷺ.

Thank you, the love of my life, Mrs Fautimah Amin. I would also like to thank one of my best friends for the last 45 years, Omar Mimrah, for your support and dedication in helping to complete this book. We couldn't have completed this effort without your help and support.

May Allah bless and guide all those who read or saw this book. May it be a guide to truth, righteousness, and happiness. Thank you sister Zarinah and Yumnah for your valuable input in making the book a reality. May Allah be with you all. Ameen

GLOSSARY

Al Ma'rifa—Certain knowledge of Allah
Al-muhsineen—The doers of good
Al hamdulillah—All thanks is due to Allah
'Asr—Afternoon prayer
As-Salamu Alaykum—May Allah's peace be upon you
Da'ee—Person who invites others to Islam
dawah—Inviting people to Islam
Deen—Spiritual wealth
Dhikr—A form of devotion typically associated with Sufism
Dhuhr—Midday prayer
Dunya—Worldly life
Fajr—Dawn prayer
Fitna—A trial of faith or practice
Fitra—The natural order of things
Haram—Holy place, different from haraam, which means forbidden
Iblees—Shaytan, the devil, Satan
Ihram—Special clothing worn on the Hajj
In-sha-Allah—If God wills
Isha—Evening prayer
Jinns—Beings created from smokeless fire whose existence is different from that of men
Khalifas—Rulers

Maghrib—Dusk or sunset prayer
Masha-Allah—Praise God. It has been the will of God.
Muhajireen—The Muslims who migrated to Madinah
Muhsineen—Those who do good
Nafs—Self
Qadar—Pre-Ordinance
Qamees—Shirt
Qibla—Compass that points towards Makkah
Quraysh—Powerful tribe in the time of
the Prophet—peace be upon him
Raka'at—Divisions of prayer
Sadaqah—Charity
Salah/salawat—Obligatory prayer
Shura—Consultation
Sirat al-mustaqeem—The straight path
SubhanAllah—Praise God
Surahs—Chapters of the Qur'an
Takbir—God is great
Ta'leem—Islamic education
Taqwa—Fear or knowledge of God
Tawheed—Worshiping only one God, the Creator
Wudhu—Ritual washing before prayer

WITNESSES' STATEMENTS

"**I AM HAPPY TO SHARE** my memories of the author Khalid Amin and the other amazingly dedicated and effective Muslim religious propagators as I saw them through the eyes of a child and later as a young adult. Growing up in New York City during the 1960s and 1970s was an eventful time. As a child, I recall seeing television footage of the civil rights movement, the activities of Dr. Martin Luther King Jr., and the Vietnam war. My family educated us about what being Black in America meant. We knew our people were not treated fairly and we also knew that some whites could be very angry and brutal towards Blacks, commonly called colored or negroes at that time. I remember seeing my mother's body seemingly broken as she sat on her bed limply sobbing with unyielding grief when she heard that our hero, Dr. Martin Luther King, Jr. had been murdered in Tennessee. I also recall riding down south to family reunions and seeing a huge official roadside billboard that read *Stop Integration and Communism—A Message from your Local Klu Klux, Klan*. As a child, I felt unsafe in our world and was very much afraid.

There were, however, some voices that made me feel reassured. The voices were those of the so-called "Black Muslim" movement. I played my mother's records of speeches by Malcolm X and I looked at the books and newspapers promoted by The Nation of Islam (NOI). Those messages made me feel more secure. I knew that despite the sad state of affairs in our country, there were strong Black men among us who were courageous and they were definitely not afraid. My uncle had joined the Nation of Islam—which we called "the Nation"—in 1967. *Muhammad Speaks* newspapers and their leader's book, *A Message to the Blackman*, were always around our house somewhere.

When we traveled about through the boroughs of New York City, we were often approached by Elijah Muhammad's street messengers who were the newspaper salesmen that brought his teachings directly to our minds. Although we tried to avoid them, these men were like the guardian angels of the neighborhood. They selflessly gave their lives and livelihoods to the mission of dawah or spreading the word of Islam to the poor neighborhoods of the United States of America. Later, when I became a Muslim, I came to know these brave missionaries and expert dawah men as *the Couriers*.

All of the adult men within the Nation were considered as part of the para-military force of the Nation of Islam. This black army was identified as the *Fruit of Islam* or the *FOI*. These men were given a quota of 300 *Muhammad Speaks* newspapers to sell each week and were held accountable for these sales as doing their share of saving our people from what they called the grave. An inspired few of the FOI were so passionate about serving their people with a message they deemed to be life-saving that they went far beyond the minimum 300 paper sales requirement, selling thousands of papers weekly instead. These men's swift-footed steps and captivatingly lyrical voices hugged the street corners of the black communities of New York and the country. They traveled in cars and vans from state to state reassuring the black children and adults of our era that we had leadership and we would be okay. We knew their leader Elijah had a plan and we didn't have to be afraid. To black children, they were our Justice League, our superheroes sailing through the retail sidewalks among the shoppers to greet the people and offer them a glimpse of a new life that could be possible for our people.

These men were special. They were sharp, clean, respectful, and very intelligent. If you were snagged into a conversation with one of them you'd likely soon be heading to the temple (later mosque) to attend the next meeting. You'd at least have purchased their Muslim newspaper. They were simply irresistible.

"Young Lady!" a voice warmly snapped into your ears and then with a smooth gesture, folded swiftly with precision and sightless manual dexterity, that Muslim newspaper would be somehow magically creased and under your arm! It was as if an elegant street ballet were being performed. They engaged you as they taught you about your history, eating a clean diet, raising strong healthy children, and having pride in yourself. You somehow knew they truly loved our people. They were confident in their teachings and they definitely were not afraid. If you didn't plan to buy that paper on that day, you'd surely be wise to walk around the block or across the street to avoid them. They were simply experts at pulling you into their spiritual space.

I eventually joined the Nation of Islam at the tender age of twelve years old shortly after my two brothers joined who were fifteen and sixteen years old at the time. The Vietnam war had recently ended, drugs were starting to take hold within our communities and African American youngsters were testing out all sorts of new ways of expression towards social change. Our parents looked on without much resistance when we converted, perhaps just glad we were entering an organization whose edicts invited a sense of old-fashioned, clean living. When Elijah Muhammad passed away in 1975, the Nation of Islam was lead by his son, Imam Warith Deen Muhammad, who began teaching what is considered orthodox Islam as opposed to the rhetoric of Black superiority previously taught by the Nation of Islam.

The leadership of Imam Muhammad was welcomed by the Couriers and the new teachings ignited a brand new fire of commitment among the ranks of the full-time newspaper salesmen. Perhaps the transition to authentic Islam as a purely scripturally-based, social reform strategy provided a much more solid message for these street couriers as it offered their African American prospects a brand new sense of religious belonging and community.

Changes in religious teachings came very quickly after Elijah Muhammad passed. Historians noted this mass conversion of the NOI membership to orthodox Islam under the leadership of Imam W. Deen Muhammad as being a most remarkable social phenomenon within our modern history. In my opinion, the Couriers had an enormous role in stabilizing the Black Muslim community during this extensive transition. They didn't seem to question the value of the changed teachings. As if they'd been waiting for these changes, they were fired up! The Couriers seemed to immediately embrace the essential Islamic message of the Oneness of God and the equality of man; even ahead of the rest of the congregation. Perhaps by being among everyday people, day-in and day-out, they'd gained a special sense as to what kind of messages were truly necessary to uplift the minds of the downtrodden.

DAWAH

These street messengers had been spit on, attacked, and even shot at while doing the brave work of propagating Islam, so they knew quite well the states of minds within the Black neighborhoods. Despite these challenges they successfully brought in or "fished-in" many people to the Muslim community. Their drive to propagate Islam intensified under the leadership of Imam W. Deen Muhammad. They continued to travel selflessly from state to state to sell *Muhammad Speaks* newspapers which transitioned its name to the *Bilalian News*, then to the *AM Journal* and eventually to *Muslim Journal*. They boldly propagated the Islamic faith, some even quitting their jobs to answer Imam W. Deen Muhammad's call to "Remake The World!" Imam W. Deen Muhammad's appreciation of their service was publicly noted as he emphatically proclaimed that his couriers were more valuable to him than his ministers! In gratitude, Imam Muhammad personally named the author, Khalid Amin, and several other couriers with Islamic names befitting the excellent human characteristics he saw in them.

In later years, the duties for propagation fell more to the local imams as official prayer leaders within our various mosques or masjids. Within that role, we've seen varying degrees of effectiveness with continuing the tradition of dawah or propagation. The role of da'ee or missionary is a very special prophetic tradition that I hope is not lost and pray this book will document and preserve. To date, I have not yet seen the level of skill nor success for sharing and propagating the religion of Al-Islam that I witnessed as a youngster among those couriers who I saw as brave supermen who gave hope and courage to me as a child growing up in New York City. There are only a precious few of these highly skilled practitioners still around today, and fewer still of their proteges who can replicate the delicate art of sharing knowledge of the Islamic faith in the manner that inspired so many to join the Muslim community's mission of healing our world.

In 2016 while in Washington, D.C., I saw a man selling a *Muslim Journal* newspaper while standing in front of a masjid. In a quick moment of observation and intimate recall, I could tell this man had been trained by a courier who was a dawah master. I called my children around that man to watch him perform the expert sales techniques that I remembered from my childhood. I asked the Muslim brother about his unique skills. He said he had once worked closely alongside the author, Khalid Amin. I was not surprised."

—Coral "Amatullah" Qadar

....

**Fautimah Amin's testimonial regard-
ing her husband, Khalid Amin:**

"I must admit this was hard for me. It took me a long time to start, and I am not sure you will understand everything I have to say here. Perhaps you could read it a few times if you are so inclined. It is not that I am so worthy of the re-read so much as it is the subject matter. I thank you for your patience.

Anyone who knows us, knows it is hard to tell exactly where one of us begins and the other ends. We are completely opposite and the same. We complement each other in that we are almost completely different in our areas of expertise, so each fills in for the other's shortcomings. We complete each other in that our philosophical passions are almost identical: love of God (Allah), love of doing good works, love of our children, even the ones who came from other parents, love of their children, love of our neighbors, and anyone else who loves the Creator, making others happy and helping others see that, whatever happens, everything is okay.

There is little we do that does not require each of us to apply our unique skill set to complete the job. So we work together in almost everything. But most people do not see it. One takes the forefront, the other works from behind. For us, it works.

So this was hard for me because it is a little like writing about myself while writing about someone else. As my son would say, "Does that make sense?"

I first saw Khalid in a dream. I could see him clearly except for his face. It was a bright white light. I could see he was waiting for me. So I began to look for him.

We married three weeks to the day after we met. We moved from Michigan (where I was living) to Texas a day later. Our whole marriage has been that much of a whirlwind.

When we married, I was Sufi. Two days after we married, he asked me about the dhikr (recitation) I was doing after the morning and evening prayers every day. It was called a *wird* and had been given to me by my sheikh. He asked me what it was. I told him it was the *wird*. He asked me where he could find it in the Qur'an. I told him I had not seen it mentioned there. He asked me where he could find it in the Hadith. I told him I had not seen it mentioned there. Based on those 3 simple questions and answers, I left Sufism and committed to following Qur'an and authentic Hadith to guide my behavior. That is how powerful his approach is. It is as if he is just showing you what you already know is true and just hadn't put your finger on.

My husband excels at education and common sense. How much of that is the strength of Islam and how much is his presentation of the facts is not really a fair question. Why? Because his presentation is the presentation of Islam itself.

So together we have worked hard to establish many things over the years, thanks to our Creator. My father always called my mother an idealist and himself a realist. Based on my life's journey, the reality is that the ideal will be real if you treat it with the respect the ideal deserves. Faith has more than 70 branches, but it is still faith, not faith in superstitions. Faith in the reality that *is* ideal.

God is so far above everything He is attributed with. He has no one like Him; He has no family. He reigns alone with no need of an inheritor (as if He might die), a partner (as if He needs someone to complete His shortcomings), a helper (as if He needs help), anyone to be a go-between (as if He has trouble hearing anything at all). HE HAS NO NEEDS. He is kind enough to meet our every necessity without it increasing or decreasing Him in any way.

The same things that happened in the time of the Prophet ﷺ continue to happen today. The rich are deceived into believing that they deserve whatever they want, they are entitled to use any means to get it, and it does not matter that those they take it from have little or nothing because they believe those people did not deserve it anyway. Scheming, treachery, lying, stealing, depriving others of their freedom, forcing others to work under shameful conditions while taxing them mercilessly; these are the hallmarks of the unjust rich and powerful.

Iblees (who became Shaytan) defied God's (Allah's) order to prostrate himself to Adam. The angels were ordered to make this prostration and at the time of the order, Iblees was among the angels so the order applied to him as well. When he defied the order, God cursed him to Hell. Instead of immediately repenting, or at least denouncing his act and working to improve himself, he doubled down by saying he was sure that Adam and his children did not deserve this high status and that he would tempt them to follow him (Shaytan) to their own destruction. God replied that Shaytan was welcome to have anyone who followed him. The ideal is to stay in constant vigilance against Shaytan and to follow only God and those who u follow Him.

God did not accept Cain's (Qabil's) sacrifice because it was not sincere. Abel (Habil) selected the best of his possessions and offered it for sacrifice with all sincerity. Qabil rewarded his brother with the first murder between men. This act, every time it is practiced, is attributed back to Qabil as the initiator of this heinous sin. In contrast, the ideal is to feel and act with sincerity.

So, the unjust rich are working with all zeal to earn their own destruction. Those who have wealth believe they are in possession of what Allah owns. Doing harm with the power they were granted will harm their own souls—may Allah protect us. Doing good with our fortunes will result in Allah rewarding us at all times every day.

> *This is the Book about which there is no doubt, a guidance for those conscious of Allah. Who believe in the unseen, establish prayer, and spend out of what We have provided for them, And who believe in what has been revealed to you, [O Muḥammad], and what was revealed before you, and of the Hereafter they are certain [in faith]. Those are upon [right] guidance from their Lord, and it is those who are the successful.—Qur'an 2:2–5*

Like any good book written for students who want to improve themselves, this book was brought to us by a teacher; a teacher who confirmed the message and the veracity of all the teachers who came before him. A teacher who, unlike all the others, was sent to all the worlds, not only his own people, and was sent to be the last messenger from Allah signaling the imminence of the Day of Judgment.

Give charity in adversity and good times. Restrain your anger. Pardon all men. Allah loves the muhsineen (God fearing people). Do not hurry off after prayers, rather, wait and bask in their benefits. Walk to the place of prayer. Make your ablutions, even when it is difficult. Spread the salaams. Feed the poor. Pray at night while others sleep. After you finish one prayer, wait for the next and pray again. Be from the righteous few. There is no need to follow the crowd.

Know that God (Allah) is in control and is absolutely worthy of our trust and our worship. I have borne witness to that truth so many times and in so many ways I cannot even count them.

Doing extreme good can be as little as removing something from the road, smiling, or sharing a drink of water.

And as I always taught my sons, "Keep your eye on the prize and don't get stuck in the mudddd." What is the prize? It is pleasing Allah and going to Jannah. What is the mudddd? It is the worldly life.

So why is all this important to say in an introduction to the man, Khalid Amin? Because he has been my teacher for nearly 40 years, and these are some of the most important things I learned during my privileged years spent married to him.

Thank you for your kind attention.

—Fautimah Doumbouya-Amin

"Shaykh Khalid has a proven track record in giving dawah (invitations) all over the USA and abroad. He is a quiet man and excellent listener. I have known him for over 40 years to be kind, generous, wise, and sincere in helping to heal people from many spiritual illnesses.

We pray to Allah that this dawah work will be a benefit to all of humanity (Muslims and non-Muslims), and on the Day of Judgment be a benefit for Shaykh Khalid Amin. Ameen."

—Imam Neelain Muhammad

Muslim African American, 4th Degree Black Belt in Jujitsu, Original Courier and Da'ee since 1973, Friend and Student of Shaykh Khalid Amin

---

"I am Harun Amin and have been giving dawah with my father since I was seven years old (1990). Ever since I can remember, I have known Shaykh Khalid Amin (my father) to be extremely adamant about calling to Allah. There are very few people that I have met on the face of the earth who talk about calling to Allah in every single conversation and just about every single sentence. Khalid Amin is one of the people with such qualities; qualities that keep Allah in the heart and call to Allah on the tongue.

My journey with Shaykh Khalid Amin has been so fruitful that I could write an entire book about the lessons and benefits regarding dawah that I've received from this amazing man. I remember him traveling around from state to state, trying to establish an Islamic institute for the indigenous Muslims in America. Although he found some small Islamic institutes, he had a difficult time finding any established institutes that taught Islam purely based on the traditions of the Prophet ﷺ.

I remember him heading to Michigan to establish a school, which started in the basements of the community members (primarily his basement). I remember the countless numbers of children he raised and taught, and I remember numerous people coming to Islam before it was the popular thing to do. I remember the vast amount of people whom my father would meet on the street and invite into our home for a meal. We so rarely ate dinner without multiple guests, that it felt strange if nobody was over for dinner. I remember many times when people stayed over for the night, people who we may not have known very well, but needed a place to stay or were just tired after a good meal.

I remember my father going out to various places that he would call his office. Such locations were literally right in the middle of the public sidewalk. He would stand there every day passing out fliers about Allah. The only days he wouldn't be at such places would be when he was sick, traveling, or dealing with another community issue. I remember meeting countless non-Muslims in my father's office downtown, only later to see the same people praying in the front row of the masjid.

I remember the number of people who came to him for help. But, even with his limited resources, he would never turn anyone away, regardless of who they were or what their struggles had been. I remember him saying, "Many people believe dawah is getting people into Islam. But, that ain't dawah, because just as fast as they come in, if they don't see it in the people, they'll leave."

Ever since his migration to Madinah in 2001, the Michigan community has genuinely missed him. Nobody has ever been able to fill his shoes on the streets of Michigan, selflessly caring for others and calling them to Allah. Until this day in 2019, people still ask about him when I walk down the streets of Ann Arbor. His level of passion and compassion are rarely seen nowadays. Although what I am saying may seem like an exaggeration because we know all community members have faults on the inside, my father, whom I can testify for, is better on the inside than what he shows on the outside.

I know him as a man committed, giving it his all, even giving his clothes for people in need. He is generous without having much, studious without having time, hard-working but sharing his wealth. He is committed without needing gratitude from anyone, loving the people and wanting people to hear the truth about Allah. He is humble, not boastful, trying to build a community when the odds against building a community were great. I remember him as a father, brother, uncle, grandfather, advisor, mentor, teacher, companion, example, workout partner, and my best friend. Many people may know my father from the outside looking in. But, I tell you as his oldest son, throughout my time of giving dawah, I have never met a da'ee (caller to Allah) as real, dedicated, courteous, gentle, skilled, wise, and effective as my father. He is beautiful both inside and out, and he would utilize the most basic principles and apply such principles to real life. May Allah bless him and give him the highest level of Jannah. Ameen."

—Harun Amin

Shaykh Khalid Amin is my father and one of the people I always looked up to. He has had a strong, positive impact on my life and many others.

Since I was young (1990), I've always known my father to be one who led by example and didn't talk much. He only taught a few classes a week, but one thing he did every day was talk and interact with people to educate them about Islam. He seemed to give them a sense of belonging. He made them feel like they had a family. When people needed assistance, he did his best to connect them to those who could assist. Sometimes, people needed a place to stay, and he would have them stay at our house, even though they weren't Muslims. People loved him so much and wanted to be around him. They wanted some of what he had. I think this is because he showed genuine love to all, regardless of their background.

My father also dedicated most of his time to studying, practicing, and teaching Islam. Our living room was filled with Islamic books that he read all the time. Most of the books were in Arabic on multiple Islamic topics. I remember that when he gave his Friday sermons, he used Shaykh Muhammad Al-Amin Al-Hararri's (who is his teacher and now my father-in-law) explanation of the Qur'an (a 32-volume book). He usually read from it every day. He also read Istithkaar and Tamheed, which are commentaries on Imam Malik's Muwatta' by Ibn Abdul Barr, and many other books. As an example of practicing what he learned, even though he was interacting with all types of people downtown in Ann Arbor, Michigan, he never shook a woman's hand. I remember Abdullah Nafees (a longtime friend of my father) said that he used to watch my father when my father couldn't see him. Nafees wanted to know if he would inappropriately interact with any women. Nafees said that Shaykh Khalid was always clean and never did any dirt. The few classes he taught were mostly on Islamic Monotheism and Creed. He had a class one day a week at several different universities, which were organized by a few of the students. From what I can remember, a lot of people came into Islam from these classes. My father, to me, was a modern-day example of an ideal Muslim.

As a father, Shaykh Khalid Amin was always concerned about his children's Islamic spiritual health. Did they pray? Did they do their Qur'an? He and my mother made the ultimate sacrifice for their children (my brothers and myself) to learn Islam. When I was about six years old, my dad took us to Morocco so that we could learn the Qur'an. We had little money and limited resources. I remember that they had total dependence on Allah. They wanted their children to be safe from the fitna (trial of faith) of North America; they put their trust in Allah and moved because that was what they felt was best. Six years and much sacrifice later, we all came back to the US with the entire Qur'an memorized. All praise is due to Allah.

As a grandfather, he always checks on his grandkids. He continually asks us if the children are doing the Qur'an or learning deen. He also contacts his old friends all over the world to check on them and to continue to give them dawah. He continues to study, act on what he learns, and spread the blessed word of Allah. He is a man who has dedicated all he owns for this purpose and stayed the course through and through.

I pray Allah continues to bless my parents. I ask Allah to give them long lives with good health and obedience to Allah. I pray Allah allows my father to write and publish many books regarding his experience in dawah and life so that many generations can benefit from his life's work, Aameen."

—Abdullah M. Amin

"To understand the magnitude of any people who were conquered and stripped of the knowledge of God, religion and self, you have to know how they evolved from a lower position in society to a higher level. After being all but destroyed and delivered to circumstances which leave you no choice but to accept whatever your conqueror says is your fate, how do you get out from under such a cruel taskmaster, who never intends to give you freedom, justice nor equality? We realized that our deadened state physically, spiritually, and mentally precluded our chances to compete intellectually, scientifically, economically, and militarily because that same oppressor invariably held us back from any glimmer of opportunity. Giving dawah all over the world changed that disadvantage.

I know, as a companion of Shaykh Khalid, and the first person to be with him from the beginning (1972), that this book is the living proof of the dawah which brought to life everything it touched in its path."

—Dr. Omar Mimrah

....

"I've always realized after meeting and picking up the sword of truth with Shaykh Khalid that giving dawah is an institution and an instrument."

—Dr. Abdullah Nafis—may Allah have Mercy on him.

....

"I am Al-Hajj Jaami Saifullah Muhammad, and for over 40 years (1975), I've had the blessing and opportunity to soldier with Shaykh Khalid Amin. Our experiences have expanded and covered over five continents. I've never had the chance to work with anyone better at calling and inviting people to Allah and His Messenger than Imam Khalid. It would take volumes to talk about or explain where we've been and what we've been able to do with Allah's help. In the interest of time and space, I will focus on one project, Masjid Tauba.

Masjid Tauba, which was established in the 1990s and remained open until 2007 (when we had to close it), gave its members a new experience and showed them the wisdom of the invitation to Islam. The community of Masjid Tauba provided the infrastructure to maintain all of the many new shahadas that we were blessed to give. For the most part, we who are now the elders that established Masjid Tauba were former members of the Nation of Islam. The new converts were practically at Masjid Tauba day in and day out, learning the fundamentals of Islam in words and righteous actions. Because many of the new converts were indigenous people, many stayed at Masjid Tauba, relishing in the environment. They not only took shahada and accepted Islam, but they also got the opportunity to live it. They learned more about Islam because they observed it in practice every day. Even today, I run into people who share how much they miss Masjid Tauba.

When we celebrated Eid, we gathered for the prayer, feast and festivities on the same day. With most of the new converts, their families were not Muslim. So being in America, they did not feel left out when so many of the immigrant Muslims could visit their families, because we were family at our masjid. We would make it an all-day celebration and have gifts, games, and presents for the children.

Under Imam Khalid's leadership, we established Jummah prayer at Eastern Michigan University in Ypsilanti and the University of Michigan in Ann Arbor. We also had weekly "Introduction to Islam" programs on Michigan State's campus in East Lansing, where we had many converts. In our dawah efforts, we serviced many prisons in the state of Michigan. I have not witnessed a program like that since Imam Khalid relocated to Madinah for good. If people were to learn just a little about what happened at Masjid Tauba and try to implement some of that knowledge into their lives, it would give them a better idea of what Muslims and Islam are all about. It is unbelievable how many people know Imam Khalid. Every time we travel or visit places, people recognize him and show deep and personal love for him. Many scholars and people who serve Islam around the world, including me, have been enriched by the opportunity to be around Imam Khalid.

I would like to tell you one of the many stories we experienced with Imam Khalid. We were coming back from Arafat on Hajj, and an older man on Hajj with us said he would like a cold drink of water. At that time, there was no refrigeration on Hajj. That particular Hajj, we walked every step of the way. When we reached a spot in Muzdalifah, two pilgrims were standing there. Their ihrams (special clothing worn on the Hajj) were the whitest you had ever seen. Their hair was midnight, silky black. It did not look like they had any signs of fatigue or of being on Hajj. They happened to have a thermos. They told us to buy some water and then to pour it into the thermos. There was a block of ice in the thermos. We drank until we almost got sick. We thanked them and they walked off. We asked some of the brothers with us to inquire as to who they were. The brothers looked, but couldn't find them. It was like they disappeared. Who they were, Allah knows best.

We ask Allah to bless us with a good ending and to keep us obeying Him and His Messenger, Ameen. We know the primary keys are to learn the deen, live it, and invite others. It was the way of the prophets from Adam, the first, to Muhammad, the last. May Allah grant them both prayers and blessings, Ameen."

—Al-Hajj Jaami

"Receiving guidance from the elderly is a key element of success. Instead of learning a life lesson after years of mistakes, poor judgment, and lack of experience, we can get a piece of advice from our elderly that can change our lives for good. I learned a lot of lessons in life the hard way and wish I had known them earlier in life so I would be in a better position today.

My life was going good or at least I thought it was going good, until I met Shaykh Khalid. Being around him brought about a critical change in my perspective. His teachings rearranged my priorities and his kind advice felt like medicine at the time of desperate need. On top of that, he wasn't asking for any exchange of benefits. Such a selfless attitude was surprising for me especially in this time and age. I really wanted to know where all this selfless generosity was coming from. What was the source of this wisdom and calmness in such a turbulent world?

Once, I asked Shaykh Khalid, were you always like this? He said he wasn't like this before, but putting his religion before everything else made him who he is. It's all about Islam and how serious we are about our deen. I learned from him that I have to make Islam my number one priority, regardless of the circumstances. And by only trying to be a good Muslim, a lot of things in my life that seemed impossible before became a piece of cake. As Shaykh Khalid would always say, "Allah's in charge." Allah's mercy has no limits and includes everything, even His beloved worshippers!

I read in a book written by Shaykh Khalid's teacher that a father brings a child into this world but a teacher takes the child to Paradise through Islamic teachings. I read, lived, and verified this piece of information. I am sad that I don't have a son yet to be around Sheikh Khalid to learn as much as he can. At the same time, I am relieved that Sheikh Khalid wrote a book for everyone to benefit from.

—Sultan Khalil of Madinah

CHAPTER 1

IMPORTANT DAWAH ADVICE

1.1 Excellence in the Invitation to Heal

THIS IS A SOCIAL WORK analysis of 50 years of experience designed to help other human beings heal from physical, mental, and spiritual illnesses. I first intended it for Muslims who are inviting humanity to Islam, but I later realized the benefits it might offer all human beings. This book contains valuable lessons from religious stories and my dawah experiences. Here you will find over 100 dawah points which will help you deal with people of all nationalities, races, and languages. These points are keys to opening up both physical and spiritual locked doors.

The path to knowledge of our Creator and understanding others contains these qualities:

Tolerance	Concern	Love
True Compassion	Short Stories	Kindness
Attention	Focus	Advice
Awareness	Faithfulness	Wisdom
Change—Within and Without		Loyalty
Learning to harmonize with others		Care

To become an excellent inviter to Islam, we must first start increasing our iman (faith), which comes in time. Conviction first begins in the heart, then Islam is made manifest through our body's actions, like when we pray, fast, etc. The principles of faith are six:

- Belief in the oneness of Allah
- Belief in His angels
- Belief in His books
- Belief in His messengers
- Belief in the Day of Judgment
- Belief in predestination

However, there are over seventy-six branches. The Companions of the Prophet Muhammad ﷺ said in a sound hadith,

> We used to be with the Prophet ﷺ when we were youths. We learned iman (faith) before we learned the Qur'an. Then we learned the Qur'an, and we were increased in Iman.—Sunan Ibn Majah 61

Today as Muslims, we are teaching the Qur'an before we teach iman. This hadith also shows us that iman has to be taught and learned. Beliefs and actions are inseparable.

Iman (belief) contains the foundation for our success in this life as well as the next. However, faith is such a broad topic that it requires training.

There is a hadith that talks about the branches of iman in Sunan Al-Nasai. Abu Huraira reported from the Messenger of Allah ﷺ that he said,

Iman has seventy-something branches of faith, and shyness is a branch of faith.

The actual Arabic word used is bid'un (بضع) means three to nine. So when the Prophet ﷺ said seventy something (بضع) it meant a number between seventy-three and seventy-nine branches of faith. This word, branches, can also be explained as qualities. This hadith is referring to actions that are in accordance with Islamic traditions, and they are called iman.

Iman increases with the performance of righteous deeds or diminishes in our disobedience. From the Qur'an, we know Allah has told us to do the things He and His Prophet ﷺ have ordered and leave the actions He and His Prophet ﷺ have prohibited. So what we have been instructed to do by Allah and His Prophet ﷺ we do, and what we have been prohibited from, we avoid.

This is the essence of iman. All the branches of faith consist of either the actions of the heart, tongue, or body. Faith and all its branches speak to our connection with the Creator. Actions of the heart include such things as the articles of faith and sincerity. Actions of the tongue include reading Qur'an and avoiding vain and idle talk. Actions of the body include making our formal prayers and being modest in our clothing choices. God willing, we will write another book that examines these branches in detail soon. This topic is of vital importance.

1.2 Dawah, the Lost Art

It has been my observation that da'ees today are passionate for the religion. They may have received formal Islamic education and others informally. However, they have not been sufficiently exposed to masters of the craft. We know from Islam, the importance of the teacher in bringing the book (theoretical knowledge) to life. With fewer and fewer people who have been trained to give dawah, fewer and fewer people have access to the knowledge.

1.3 Why Is it So Important to be an Inviter to the Lord of All the Worlds?

This section is dedicated to sharing what I have learned over the years about spiritual healing for both myself and others. Here, I want to introduce you to why giving dawah is so important for every Muslim and to help you see the benefit of studying how it is done and why.

Inviting people to Allah is the work of all the messengers from Adam to Muhammad. This includes such prominent messengers as Abraham, Isaac, Jacob, and Jesus. Our job is to reconnect people with their Lord. Sometimes the world gets us so distracted that we lose sight of what is essential, even our health. This is a significant loss since our connection with our Lord is the most precious thing we have.

As an inviter (da'ee), the work is healing for both the patient and the healer. It helps us control our tempers and desires and develops humility and a spirit of service to humanity.

Another benefit is that you will come to appreciate how complicated personal problems can be. You may find others' problems affect their physical health until they are tied up in knots. Seeing their problems will help you understand how your issues are not as severe as you thought they were.

This work will also relieve spiritual burdens you may have been carrying around for years. It gives you keys to hidden things you may not have known about yourself as well as an understanding of human nature.

A person can find themselves more tolerant and with more love and genuine concern for people, regardless of their backgrounds. It can motivate you and build up your spirit to help others through their crises as well as your own.

This work will allow you to make one paradigm shift after another, allowing you to see life through other lenses as it unfolds for people you meet and as it unfolds for yourself. As you and your perspectives evolve, so will your ability to see situations and evaluate them wisely.

The more involved you become, the more you will see you are not only dealing with bodies, but you are dealing with souls. dawah allows you to see, feel, and taste the pain and hurt of other human beings.

It will deliver you a natural high if you are sincere. A genuine person will find many locked doors unlocking, both spiritual and physical. Unexpected opportunities will unfold before your very eyes.

This work is fun and can lead you to rediscover your sense of humor. It can be very humorous.

Also, be aware that this work can reveal the wickedness that exists in the world and people. You will see the manifestation of the work of Satan himself. He will do all that he can to stop you from continuing this work because he is opposed to it.

Finally, this work will bring you closer to your Lord. It will elevate your status with Him. The help you need will manifest from all directions. You will find outlets and exits that you could never imagine. It will give you extraordinary patience and take you over the top.

Doing this work will make you a spiritual ambassador of the Lord of all the Worlds.

CHAPTER 2

SOUL FOOD

2.1 Remember Allah is the Ultimate Reality

REMEMBER THAT ALLAH, THE LORD of all the Worlds, is the ultimate reality. Naturally, everyone is dealing with their worldly realities. Most of us have wives or husbands, boyfriends or girlfriends, children, mothers and fathers, friends, and relatives. Work, paying bills, engaging in normal daily activities, all of these things keep us busy with the world. All of these worldly realities are temporary. Some of these worldly realities can bring us closer to our Lord. Others can drown us in the well of ignorance. Our mothers and fathers won't live forever; neither will our sisters, brothers, children, friends, and other relatives. When everyone and everything dies, only Allah, the Ever-Living, will remain. He is the ultimate reality. This life is short; fifty to ninety years and we die. What happens after death? That's when the ultimate reality kicks in. Everything in this world is temporary. Allah is Eternal. He will never die.

Remember that Allah is the only reality. Is it healthy to think, "Others should work in the field of dawah while I concentrate on in-house, masjid teaching, and university lectures because I'm on a different level as an Islamic Scholar?" The Prophet ﷺ and his Companions were actively giving dawah in the field. Are we better than them? Leaders should be out front in their actions. This is one of the problems in the world today. Political and religious leaders have a problem not knowing how to connect with the common man. We all, regardless of our status, need to be working in the field. It will only help to purify us and bring us closer to Allah and give us an understanding of the ordinary people. People are in dire need of help including physical, spiritual, and mental support, especially in this day and age.

My reality as a child changed when I was 16 years old. I used to say that I couldn't wait until I was old enough to leave home and live on my own. My mother used to say that the grass always looks greener on the other side of the fence. When I left home I had to face the many realities of life like paying rent, lights, cleaning my clothes, and the house. I said to myself that it wasn't all that bad when I lived at home.

At 21 and 25, even more significant changes happened, and my world began to expand even more. At 27, I left America to study in Makkah. Wow, what a different world! It was like being dropped on another planet. At the age of 33, I returned to America, got married, and my wife began to have children. Now, at 60, everyone is grown. Also, at the first writing of this book, I have 23 grandchildren with some on the way.

Still, my reality is continuously changing as I am living in Madinah, in the land of our Beloved Prophet Muhammad ﷺ. Understanding Allah being the ultimate reality is becoming clearer by the second. Who knows whether we have 10, 20, 30, 40 or 50 years remaining in our lives. We are trying to prepare ourselves to meet Allah. No one knows that hour but Him. There is a beautiful Muslim brother in Masjid al-Nabawi who is over 120 years old, masha'Allah.

He prays five salawat daily in the Haram. He also walks to the Haram daily.

Inviters to Allah, remember our reality isn't the ultimate reality. Allah is the Ultimate Reality for all of humanity. Let us be diligent in inviting humanity to the Ultimate Reality, Allah.

As callers to Allah, we must have our values, and we must understand that other people have values too. I can remember hearing my father telling my mother to stay out of my sister's and her husband's business. He said that if they ask for advice, we give it to them, but let them work out their problems. He said that if her husband hits her, then he would immediately enter their affair. These were some of my father's values.

Another time, I remember visiting my mother's brother when we were children. I don't remember what happened, but my uncle's wife disrespected my father. He told my mother, "If you want to visit your brother I won't stop you, but if they're going to see me, then they must come to my house and visit me. I'm not going to visit them again."

We must have values and stand by them. Respect other people's values even if you don't agree with them. There are personal values, and there are also family values. I can remember when I was a child, the adults used to say children should be seen and not heard. They used to say, "Spare the rod and spoil the child." I remember my mother asking my father to go to church on Sunday. He said, "The same God that hears you praying in the church can hear me praying in my bed. The church is full of hypocrites. They go to church on Sunday and come out worse than they were before they went in." He also said, "I pick up the church's garbage. If you picked up their garbage, you would know who they are."

The day my father was dying, they called me to come quickly to see him. I went into his room with my wife, locked the door, and we told him, "We love you, and we want to be with you for eternity in Paradise, but there is a condition."

He asked what it was.

I said, "The condition is that you believe that there is no god but Allah and that Muhammad ﷺ is His Messenger."

He said, "Repeat it."

I repeated it, and he repeated it after me. This was about 8 a.m. He died between 1 p.m. and 3 p.m. that same afternoon. May Allah forgive him, accept him and have mercy on him, aameen—my Father, George Carter from Staten Island, NY.

2.2 Stay in Consultation

Our beloved Prophet Muhammad ﷺ was known for staying in consultation within his home and amongst his companions in affairs which legislation had not been revealed. We should be in discussion within our homes, with our families, in our masjids, and our businesses. Giving dawah should keep us in consultation, always seeking advice for the pleasure of Allah. We shouldn't ever think that our opinion on a matter has more weight. If we are listening with our hearts, we will find useful, beneficial answers within our consultation. Allah guides whomever He pleases.

Even if we have been giving dawah for some years, we must humble ourselves and be open to shura (consultation). Many times answers are sent to us through others, but are we listening? The inviters to Allah must offer positive thoughts and ideas for people's minds. Encourage people to read scriptures. Encourage people to think good thoughts. We should show them by example how to help others. Positive thinking produces positive actions. The mind needs wholesome stimulation. Feed the mind, heart, and soul.

> *And it has already been revealed to you in the book (This Qur'an) that when you hear the verses of Allah being*

denied or mocked at, then sit not with them, until they engage in conversation other than that.—Qur'an 4:140

A wise person stays in consultation as often as possible because they realize that there is a limitation to their knowledge. Allah knows, and we don't know.

And those who answer the call of their Lord [i.e., to believe that He is the only One Lord (Allah) and to worship none but Him alone] and perform As-salah (Iqamat as salah) and who conduct their affairs by mutual consultation and who spend of what we have bestowed on them...—Qur'an 42:38

This verse was revealed among the Ansar (People of Madinah). The Messenger of Allah invited them to iman (faith), and they accepted it from the core of their hearts. When salah (prayer) is established, there is faith, and the religion is established. If prayer is neglected or left, then there is disbelief, and the deen (religion of the person) is destroyed.

2.3 Remember that Allah Controls Everything

We must study the story of Ayyub (Job). I will present some interesting aspects of his story here, making use of the information provided in the explanation of the Qur'an titled, *The Gardens of Bliss* by Sheikh Muhammad Amin al Harrar.

Ayyub was a patient servant of Allah because he was the son of Amawe, son of Raziq, son of Rome, son of Eesa, son of Ishaq (Isaac), son of Ibraheem (Abraham)—may Allah's peace be upon him. His mother was from the children of Lot, the son of Haran. His wife's name was Rahmah, the daughter of Afratheem, who was the son of Yusef (Joseph)—may Allah's peace be upon him. Some say his wife was Layyan, the daughter of Yaqub (Jacob)—may Allah's peace be upon him.

Ayyub lived in the time of Yaqub. It was said by al-Qurtubi that only three people believed in Ayyub. He was 93 years old. It was transmitted that he cried out to his Lord as he was sick and in severe pain. Ayyub was a man of great wealth. He was an obedient servant of Allah, who always helped the poor and orphans, so Shaytan, the devil, was envious of him because of this.

Shaytan said to Allah, "Oh my Lord, your slave Ayyub, surely you have bestowed on him your favors, and he is thankful to you. If you test him by removing these favors, you will see something different."

Allah said, "He will worship and praise Me regardless of his circumstances."

Iblees (Satan) said, "My Lord, afflict him, his children, and his wealth."

Allah told Ayyub through Jibril, "Hit your foot on the ground." The place was called al-Jabiyah, which was the land of Sham, in the area of Abi Timam. There are two reports about this history. The first report: It was said that when Ayyub (Job) hit his right foot on the ground, a spring of hot water appeared, so he washed with it. When he hit his left foot on the ground, a spring of cold water appeared and he drank from it. The second report: Hassan reported that when Ayyub stomped his foot on the ground a spring appeared so he washed with this water. Then he walked 30 feet and another spring appeared so he drank from it. Both reports give the good news that washing with the first above-mentioned spring water healed Ayyub's external sicknesses and drinking from the second spring healed his internal illnesses.

During Ayuub's trial, he lost everything. The consensus among the scholars is that his family died and were brought back to life. They also agree that he was healed from his sickness. Ibn Abbas said that Ayyub's test lasted seven years, seven months, seven days, and some hours.

The illness that afflicted Ayyub was a skin disease and it covered his entire body. This water was from a hot spring, which is excellent in healing this type of sickness. It is beneficial internally as well as externally. As we see, springs, which have appeared in different countries, are used as bathhouses. Many of these springs are in Europe, Egypt, and Ethiopia. These springs are used to treat many skin diseases externally as well as internal sicknesses like the water from Fasha, Switzerland, Halwan, Kusam, and Arr in Ethiopia.

Ayyub had thirteen family members. Allah increased their number after his trial. Ayyub's sickness was so severe that nothing remained of him except his heart and tongue. Then a worm came to his heart and began to bite him, then one came to his tongue and began to eat him. At that time, Ayyub finally called on his Lord.

In the book *Zahra Arriyad* that Ayyub had four larvae remaining on his body. Each of these was transformed into forms we know today. One of them left his body and landed on the mulberry tree and became the silkworm. A second one landed in the water and became a leech. A third one fell in grain and became a wood-worm (or moth worm). Finally, the last landed in the mountains and became a bee.

Ayyub was a patient servant of Allah who didn't complain. He asked Allah to heal him, as his whole body was sick except his tongue and heart. He was fearful for his people that Shaytan would be fitna for them by whispering to them, "If he were a Prophet then why is he being tried like this, Allah would remove this if he would call on him."

It was reported after Ayyub's affliction left him, Allah sent down from the heavens two white pieces of cloth, which he put on and walked to his house. Then a cloud came and rained gold in his wheat field until it was filled with gold. Then another cloud came and rained silver in his barley field until it was filled with silver. He thanked Allah for his wife serving him. Allah returned his wife's youthfulness and beauty.

Inviters to Allah must remember that Allah is in control of everything.

2.4 What Seems to be Far is Near

Everything that is coming is near. I can remember it like yesterday when I was 20 years old, but that was 1971. Surely time flies. Death is close to us, and only Allah knows its time. Likewise, when it seems so challenging giving dawah, and no one is responding to the call, remember that victory is near. When the truth comes, falsehood must vanish, surely lies are ever-vanishing things. Remember, Allah is in the heavens, but He is closer to us than our jugular vein. There is no victory except with Allah, the Mighty and the Wise. Give dawah with confidence, believing that Allah will accept your efforts and that, eventually, many will be guided by your work.

2.5 Are We Really Ready to Be Tested?

Our beloved Prophet Muhammad ﷺ told us that the more Allah loves you, the more He tries and tests you. No one was tested more than Allah's messengers and prophets. Through these tests, Allah molded and shaped them for their mission. Steel is put in the fire to form it and make it strong. Some of our righteous predecessors said that with patience, you will find what you want, and that taqwa (fear and reverence of the Creator) will make steel easy to bend.

Remember callers to Allah, whatever trials and tests you are going through, Allah is molding your iman (faith) to be like steel. He's only making you stronger. Bear the tests and trials and be patient. Ask Allah for His help to be steadfast. Strive to be of those who are firmly grounded in faith and knowledge. Look at the story of Abraham (Ibrahim) when he was thrown in the fire. His faith wavered not.

The Story of Abraham in the Fire

And indeed We bestowed earlier on Ibrahim (Abraham) his (portion of) guidance, for We knew him well (as to his belief in the Oneness of Allah).

When he said to his father and his people, "What are those images to which you are devoted?"

They said, "We found our fathers worshipping these idols."

He said, "Indeed, you and your fathers have been in manifest error."

They said, "Have you brought us the truth, or are you one of those who play about?"

He said, "Nay, your Lord is the Lord of the heavens and the earth who created them, and I am a witness to that.

"And by Allah, I shall plot a plan (to destroy) your idols after you have gone away and turned your backs."

So, he broke them to pieces, (all) except the biggest of them, that they might turn to it.

They said, "Who has done this to our alihah (gods)?" He must indeed be one of the dhalimun (wrong-doers)."

They said, "We heard a young man talking against them, who is called Ibrahim (Abraham)."

They said, "Then bring him before the eyes of the people, that they may testify."

They said, "Are you the one who has done this to our gods, oh Ibrahim (Abraham)?"

Ibrahim (Abraham) said, "Nay, this one, the biggest of them (idols), did it. Ask them if they can speak."

So, they turned to themselves and said, "Verily, you are the Zalimun (polytheists and wrong-doers)."

Then they turned to themselves (their first thought) and said, "Indeed you, (Ibrahim), know well that these (idols) speak not!"

Ibrahim said, "Do you then worship besides Allah things that can neither be of any benefit to you nor do you any harm?"

"Fie upon you and upon that which you worship besides Allah! Have you then no sense?"

They said, "Burn him and help your alihah (gods) if you are men of action."

We (Allah) said, "Oh fire! Be you coolness and safety for Ibrahim (Abraham)!"—Qur'an 21: 51-70

Following is the explanation of these verses:

Surely, We gave Ibrahim, before Musa and Harun, guidance. We gave him faith in Allah (iman), and the understanding of tawheed (The Oneness of Allah). Belief in Allah contains all beautiful virtues and excellent noble manners.

Ibrahim's father was named Aazara. His people were the people of Babylon in Iraq. Iraq was so named because it was on the shores of the Tigris and the Euphrates rivers.

Remember We gave Ibrahim guidance when he stood up and said to his father and his people, "What are these idols which you are worshipping?" By asking them this question, Ibrahim wanted them to ponder over their affairs. He tried to belittle them and show them the reality of their ignorance. He wanted them to think a little that those rocks and stones couldn't benefit them in the least. Some of them were made of gold, silver, steel, lead, copper, rocks, and wood. Their big icon wore a gold jeweled crown. Its two eyes were rubies that shined at night.

His people said, "We found our forefathers worshipping them." He replied, "You and your fathers are surely in manifest error." They said, "Did you come to us with the truth, or are you playing games with us?" This question was a question of amazement, or a question asked by them to distance themselves from the severe mistake that they thought he was calling them to.

Ibrahim's people had a celebration every year. When they returned from their celebration, they would visit their idols, make prostrations to them, and then return to their homes. So, Ibrahim's father told his son, "If you go to this celebration with us, you will be amazed by our religion." Ibrahim went with them, but on the way, he complained of sickness in his legs. As he lagged, and the weak ones were remaining, one of them heard him saying, "I shall plot a plan [to destroy] your idols."

So Ibrahim returned to the house where these idols were and faced the big god Bahwa, which had smaller icons next to it. The tribe used to meet at this place. They used to put food in front of these idols so it would be blessed, and they would eat it. So, when Ibrahim saw the food in front of the gods, he said to them mockingly, "Aren't you going to eat?" When they didn't answer him, he said, "What is the matter with you; you can't talk?" He said, "You have absolutely nothing," and began chopping them to pieces with an axe. Then he tied the axe on the neck of the biggest idol. Perhaps the people will return and ask the most prominent idol about who destroyed the other gods. Now, being that the icon couldn't answer them, they would know that their worship was based on ignorance.

The people asked, "Who destroyed our idols?" Some of them, who heard what Ibrahim said before, answered, "We heard a young boy saying bad things about our idols." They said, "His name is Ibrahim." This news reached the arrogant tyrant Namrood.

He said, "Bring him here so people can see him and testify against him." Ibrahim was asked, "Did you do this to our idols?"

Ibrahim replied, "The one who has the hatchet on him did it. Ask the broken idols what happened." Ibrahim wanted to show them that an idol who can't talk and doesn't have knowledge, doesn't deserve to be worshipped.

So, Namrood and his people gathered together to burn Ibrahim alive. They kept him locked up in a house, then built another residence in which they planned on burning Ibrahim alive. So they gathered wood for a month so that it could be used to burn Ibrahim. After they gathered all the wood they needed, they started a fire. The flames were so fierce and hot that any bird that flew near it was burned alive. They lit the fire and let it burn for seven days until it became scorching hot.

However, when they wanted to throw Ibrahim in the fire, they didn't know how to do it. It was said that Iblees, the Devil, came and taught them how to build a special apparatus (sling) that could throw Ibrahim into the fire. So they tied Ibrahim on this man-made sling to throw him into the blaze. Then the heavens and earth and whatever was within them like the angels cried out. They said, "Oh Allah, our Lord; Your loved one, Ibrahim, is about to be thrown into the fire, and there is no one on earth other than him who worships you. Permit us to help him.

Allah said, "This is my loved one; I have no other loved one other than him. I am his God (Deity); he has no other God besides me. If he calls on any one of you, then help him. I've permitted him to do that. And if he doesn't call on any other than Me, surely I am the Best Knower of his affairs. I am his Friend and Helper. Leave this matter between Me and him."

So when they wanted to throw him in the fire, the angel in charge of water came to him and said, "If you want me to, I can put out this fire." Then the angel in charge of air came to him and said, "If you want, I will carry this fire away with the wind."

Ibrahim said, "I don't need any of you. Allah is sufficient for me, and a blessed Protector and Guardian."

Ubay Ibn Kab reported that when they tied Ibrahim to this machine and were about to throw him into the fire, he said, "There is no God but You. Glorified are You. To You belongs all praise. There is no partner with You. To You belongs the rule, You have no partner."

Everything wanted to put out the fire except the lizard. He was blowing on the fire to increase it. "Ibrahim was thrown in the fire and remained in it for seven days. Nothing burned except for the shackles.

Ibrahim said, "The best time of my life was when I was in the fire." Jibril came down to be with him in the fire and brought him a qamees (shirt) from Paradise to wear and a rug from Paradise to sit on. He then dressed Ibrahim with the qamees, sat him on the carpet, and sat with him, talking to him and keeping him company.

After some time, Aazara, Ibrahim's father, went to Namrood and said, "Give me permission to take the remains of Ibrahim (his bones), so I can bury them." So Namrood and his people went and made a hole in the wall and saw Ibrahim sitting in a garden enjoying himself, and his clothes were wet.

He had a qamees on and was sitting on a rug with an angel sitting next to him.

Namrood called him saying, "Oh Ibrahim, surely your God has displayed His power, now can you come out of the fire."

He said, "Yes." Then Ibrahim stood up and walked until he exited from the fire.

Namrood said, "Who was that I saw sitting with you?"

Ibrahim said, "It was an angel who my Lord sent to me, to keep me company."

Namrood said, "Surely, I'm going to make a sacrifice to your God after seeing His might and power."

Ibrahim said, "He will not accept this sacrifice as long as you are upon your religion."

Namrood said to Ibrahim, "Oh Ibrahim, it is impossible to leave my rule and kingdom, but I will slaughter to Him." Then he made a sacrifice to Him, and he stopped trying to harm Ibrahim.

Why did Allah test Ibrahim—peace be upon him—with fire? Every prophet came with a miracle from Allah and was relevant to the people of his time. The people of Ibrahim worshipped fire, the sun, the moon, and stars. They believed that they were gods and that they had relevance and influence in their life. So, Allah showed them that these things do not influence their lives.

2.6 Feed the Poor

Many people are homeless and hungry. They just need a little love and some food. Prophet Muhammad ﷺ has ordered us as Muslims to feed the poor and take care of the orphans. How can we sleep with a full stomach when our neighbors or countrymen are going to bed hungry? If you feed people, they will listen to you attentively. People need solid food, as well as good wholesome spiritual food. If the stomach is full and the soul is empty, then you are spiritually starving. The soul needs food as the body needs food.

Inviter to Allah, be active in feeding other human beings regardless of their race, creed, or religion. Hasten to do good, seeking the pleasure of the Almighty Allah. "Oh humankind, all of you are poor to Allah, and He is the Mighty and the Wise. If He so willed He would take you away and bring in another creation."

I never knew what a real neighbor was until I moved into a new neighborhood in Madinah, Saudi Arabia. There was a new neighbor of ours whose husband had died. She had three children. She never cooked food except that she sent us a portion of it daily. When I looked up, she had moved. When I asked my family where she was, they told me that they lost contact with her—what a blessed neighbor. If you feed a hungry person, you can teach them.

2.7 Pray at Night While Others are Sleeping

This is one of the formulas for success. Work hard in the day inviting people to Allah and pray late at night to the Lord of the Worlds, Allah, that He opens up peoples' hearts and grants them guidance. Surely, He has power over all things.

Sincere prayer to the Lord of all the Worlds, Allah, changes things. He listens to whoever praises Him. The Creator is above His Throne, and His Throne is above the seventh heaven. Allah is above the seventh heaven with His essence, but He is everywhere with His knowledge.

In the hadith from Muwatta Imam Malik, Abu Hurayra—may Allah be pleased with him—reported that the Messenger of Allah ﷺ said, "Our Lord descends to the lowest heaven in this world on the last third of each night. Then He says, 'Whoever calls on Me, I will answer him. Whoever asks Me for something, I will give it to him. Whoever asks for My forgiveness, then I will forgive him.'"

This is a sound hadith. This is the proof as it is agreed by the consensus of the scholars that surely Allah is in the heavens on His Throne, which is above the seventh heaven. Again, Allah is above His Throne in His essence, everywhere by His knowledge. This also negates the saying that Allah Himself is everywhere and not on His Throne.

2.8 Be Watchful

There is an old saying, "Watch as well as pray." When we're on the streets giving dawah, we should be very observant. If one Muslim brother is talking, the person with him should be vigilant. Be aware of your surroundings. If you see or feel trouble coming, remember Allah. Be on the alert. If you still feel something after this, take a break. Go to prayer, read the Qur'an, or drink some tea. Allah will manifest what is going on around you in the unseen world. We must learn how to spot troublemakers and avoid them. Never be so busy you can't speak to people you know or recognize. Allah will send his angels to protect you. He will also send his servants to look out for you. Never go out and give dawah when you have fear. Allah loves brave, bold, courageous men who are humble and gentle. Be fearless without an atom's weight of pride.

CHAPTER 3

INTRODUCTION TO BEING A DA'EE

WE ARE HERE TO SERVE humanity and help them to grow and develop physically, mentally, and spiritually. We are not here to judge, ridicule, or make a mockery of people and their conditions. We must learn to overlook people's faults, weaknesses, and addictions. Our job is to find a way to people's hearts and help them heal from the many spiritual illnesses in which they suffer. Instead of us always talking, we should try to get others to express themselves, even if it sounds ridiculous. This is where we must practice learning these dawah points.

The first thing a da'ee must do is to find a quiet place and self-reflect. It is even better to do it with an experienced mentor or teacher to increase the effectiveness of this exercise. It will take time. This is also a good time to learn more about the basics. These are critical steps in preparing to deal with real-life situations and problems. Your health is vital if you are to help others heal.

The following are lessons for the prospective da'ee, starting with self-reflection. Are these qualities you already possess or is this a good starting point in the process of improving your connection with the Creator?

Lessons for the Prospective Da'ee
Self-Reflection

3.1 Faith

a. Actions of the Heart

Sincerity of intention is one of the most important things a da'ee can have for success. Oftentimes, the new da'ee will have an inappropriate intention at the beginning. This is a common problem. Sometimes, people want to be known as knowledgeable. Other times they want to make money or to be famous. It will take time to grow into the work and recognize it for what it is. It is a service to mankind for the pleasure of Allah; and no other reason.

Hasan AlBasri—may Allah have mercy on him—said, "We used to seek knowledge for worldly gain, and we were pulled to the next life."

Sufyan Atthouri and Habeeb Ibn Abi Thabit—may Allah have mercy on them—said, "We searched for this affair (spiritual knowledge), and we had no intention in it. Then, after some time, the intention came."

b. Actions of the Tongue

Our tongues are a powerful tool for spreading good or evil. The best way we as da'ees can use them is to stay in the remembrance of Allah whether through reading Qur'an or testifying to the Oneness of Allah, acquiring knowledge or asking Allah for what we need. The things we should stay away from include using our tongues to lie or backbite or to utter negative or offensive ideas.

c. Actions of the Body

There are many branches of faith connected to the actions of our bodies. We can use our hands, feet, eyes, ears, mouth, or private parts for righteousness or evil. Examples of this are washing for prayer (wudu), giving in charity, eating halal (lawful) things, comforting our parents, and assisting in noble tasks.

3.2 Humility

Why is it that when we get so-called "good jobs" or positions in society and see other Muslims on the street dressed in robes and Muslim kufis (hats), we refuse to give them salaams? Do we think our jobs and our status will save us? Why are we ashamed to be identified as Muslims? We must be proud of Islam. We should not think of ourselves as being better than others. We must be humble servants of Allah, walking softly upon the earth, which will eventually swallow us up in our graves. Inviters to Allah, tread softly. Whoever thinks they are superior has an inferiority complex, so they must make others feel bad for themselves to feel good.

As Muslims, we have been ordered to be humble servants of Allah. We should not think we are better than others. The inviter to Allah should behave with humility, with strength and conviction.

> *And turn not thy cheek away from people in [false] pride, and walk not haughtily on earth: for, behold, God does not love anyone who, out of self-conceit, acts in a boastful manner.—Qur'an 31:18*

Another example is,

> *Whatever good happens to thee is from God; and whatever evil befalls thee is from thyself. And We have sent thee [O*

Muhammad] as an apostle unto all mankind: and none can bear witness [thereto] as God does.—Qur'an 4:79

3.3 Honesty

How can we be honest with others but not with ourselves? How can we be honest with ourselves if we are not honest with the One Who created us, the Lord of all the Worlds? Charity starts at home, and then it spreads abroad. How can we know the Lord of the Worlds who we cannot see, if we don't even know ourselves who we see every day? When we realize our weaknesses and shortcomings, we will be able to understand the strengths of Allah, the Lord of the Worlds. If we are kind of famous in this life, like in sports, music or acting, people tend to be very artificial with us, always stroking our egos, filling our heads with praise and glory. Remember, all praise and glory belong to Allah, the Lord of all the Worlds.

Since we feed into these traps, it steers us into the spiritual world of delusion and dishonesty. If a person did not have money or fame, how many real friends would they have? We must be honest with ourselves. We must learn to grow spiritually on our level, not based on others' praises for us. We must look in the mirror and see our true selves. When you are honestly working on yourself, you do not have time to look at the faults of others. When people praise and glorify you, it becomes sickening and spiritually gross, because honestly speaking, you know you have a long way to go to grow spiritually. If we understood that our Lord sees and hears everything we do, we would be more honest with Him. We should not let others cut us off in our spiritual journey back to our Lord. None of those people will answer for our misdeeds on the Day of Judgment. Tend to yourself. Do not let others cause you to be deceived into neglecting your peace.

We pray Allah will bless us with honesty. This world is filled with lies and corruption.

3.4 Truthfulness

> *Oh, you who believe, fear Allah, and be with the truthful.* —Qur'an 9:119

Birds of a feather flock together. As inviters to Allah, we must be truthful within ourselves. Truth should be our demeanor. We must stand on the truth's side.

> *When the truth comes, falsehood will vanish—surely falsehood is an ever-vanishing thing.* —Qur'an 17:81

People are looking for the truth because they have been lied to all their lives. Although we must be vigilant about the facts, we should not use the truth as a stick to beat people. Be kind and gentle with it. The truth is a double-edged sword; it cuts both ways, coming and going. The Creator, Allah, is the Truth. It belongs to Him. Beware of a lie dressed in the clothes of truth. Truth rings a bell when you hear it. It is better to be poor and truthful than to be a rich liar. The truth has one face but lies have many.

3.5 Kindheartedness

> *And by the Mercy of Allah, you dealt with them gently. Had you, [Muhammad], been severe and harsh hearted, they would have broken away from you; so pass over [their faults], and ask [Allah's] forgiveness for them, and consult them in affairs. Then, when you have taken a decision, put your trust in Allah. Certainly, Allah loves those who put their trust [in Him].* —3:159

Allah is Gentle, and He loves gentleness. The inviter must be gentle and resolved.

3.6 Consideration

Inviters to Allah must be considerate. Consider other people's feelings. Consider their circumstances and conditions. Be kind to others as an act of worship, and they will eventually be attentive to you, to their spiritual benefit.

3.7 Share Your Time

Be willing to share your time with others. Time is precious. The inviter to Allah must be conscious of his time. He must be willing to give others his undivided attention. Children need a lot of attention, and so do new Muslims. They are like spiritual babies. They must be taken care of until they are spiritually mature enough to take care of themselves. For this to happen, you must continuously teach and train them as you would a child. This requires time and effort.

3.8 Patience

Nothing happens overnight. Allah has been so patient with our ignorance, so we must be patient with others. The inviter to Allah must use patience in dealing with other human beings. He must give them time to grow. Work with people on their level of understanding. It was said that with taqwa (continuous awareness of Allah's oneness and doing everything in obedience to Allah and His prophet ﷺ, you will find what you need, and with patience, you will make steel soft.

3.9 Selflessness

Being selfless is caring for others and not for oneself; it is being completely unselfish. To be a good inviter to Allah, people must truly feel that you care for them. We cannot display hatred and expect to draw people to Islam. Selflessness calls for sacrifice.

3.10 Choose Your Friends, Do Not Let Your Friends Choose You

People usually choose friends based on what they are doing or what they are into. As a result, in many cases, you are selected by a set group of people based on who you are and what you do. If a person is famous, they usually attract people who are superficially attracted to their fame and popularity. These are the kind of people who feed their egos and tend to cling to them. They are only looking to fulfill their wants and desires. Drugs, alcohol, sex, and partying seem to be the order of the day. Often, these famous people have someone who they grew up with around them, but in most cases, they are also weak spiritually, engrossed in drugs, sex, partying, etc. We can be surrounded by devils in human form and not even know it. We should choose to be around people who will encourage us to do good, be righteous; people who can appreciate us for who we are. Often, our relationships with friends are phony and immature.

Sometimes these famous people have someone around them who seems to be spiritual, but they are very shallow in understanding religious and spiritual matters. Sometimes you could want to help someone, but you must wait until the opportunity presents itself. It may take years for this to happen, but be patient and steadfast—surely, the opportunity will be brought to your doorstep. Often, people choose you to be their friend because you make them laugh, or because you attract nice looking girls. We should try to be with people who are trying to be upright, sincere, honest, respectful, and dignified.

One day when I was visiting New York, after years of being away, I saw some girls with whom I went to high school. So I asked them how they were doing. They told me they were about to get paid. I told them to slow their roll. After some years passed, I was visiting my mother in New York and saw one of these girls again and asked her about her friend. She began crying and wailing.

She said her friend was killed on 42nd St. They chopped her up in pieces and dumped her in a garbage can. She was hanging out with the wrong people and this ended disastrously. Be careful when choosing people to spend your time with, make sure they have your welfare in mind. One good friend is better than ten. If you find one real friend in your whole life, then you are blessed.

3.11 Dignity

Inviters to Allah must be dignified and not prideful. We must have self-respect and respect other human beings regardless of their physical or spiritual condition. We must have respect for human life, and we must respect human dignity irrespective of a person's religious beliefs or ideas. If we do not have self-respect, how can we respect others? Our manners should be dignified. We should have a decent appearance. Even if we only have one set of clothes, they should be cleaned and pressed. We should be groomed physically, appear wise, and spiritual. We should handle and deal with other human beings in a respectable, dignified manner.

One day there was a Muslim brother who used to give dawah. He would always say to everyone who passed him, "Good morning, have a nice day."

One day a lady passed by him and stopped. She said, "I've been passing you for the last five years, and you have been saying, 'good morning, have a nice day,' and I never answered you." She said, "I'm tired of being a bitch."

The Muslim said to her, "Don't worry, we all act like bitches from time to time."

She laughed and said, "You are something else. What do you have?" So, she bought some incense from him, and he gave her some Islamic fliers to read. Remember, it took five years of daily interaction with this woman just to get a response. Even if people reject you or make a mockery of you, keep your composure and dignity. Turn your affairs over to Allah.

CHAPTER 4

TRAINING IN THE FIELD

HAVING SPENT TIME WITH A mentor to help with self-reflection, the prospective da'ee is now ready to continue lessons with his/her teacher and to begin lessons in the field. One example of an initial lesson might be learning to approach people and help them see what you understand. Of course, in the dynamic situation the field represents, lessons may take different topics or forms from one day to the next. At the first contact, our goal here is to introduce a single thought about Islam. It is not to convince, change, or challenge. It is to plant a seed.

Approaching and coming to a meeting of the minds with people generally has 3 steps:

1. Introduction
2. Presentation
3. Closing

These are the steps generally used in sales. Here, however, what we are selling is the Truth and no tricks or gimmicks are required. These steps are about encouraging engagement and open and honest conversations.

4.1 Capture Someone's Attention with a Kind Introduction

Sometimes people are so busy with their daily lives that they don't even see what is in front of them. In giving dawah, we have an introduction, a presentation, and a closing.

For this you need to be well-equipped with a polished introduction like compliments, such as, "You look like you're well-educated", or, "That's a beautiful suit you're wearing, where did you buy it?" Another choice might be a warning for the person's safety like, "Hey, watch out for the car. It almost hit you." A kind word can encourage people to give you a bit of their attention. In these days and times, too often kindness is a rare commodity.

4.2 Presentation

As soon as your introduction is successful, you must immediately bring forth your presentation. The presentation should be only long enough to prepare for the close.

The presentation is actually business focused. We take a simple product and offer it. We can ask for a donation for items we may have like, incense, books, etc. to further our dawah cause so we can continue working and helping people in need. Our customers decide how much they give. Between the introduction and the presentation, we have two opportunities. First, we show them the manners of a Muslim. Second, we do a little light business that helps fund our ability to come back the next day and the next and the next. The presentation should last only long enough to close your sale or to make your point. We usually sell incense or something else that's a small and easy purchase for most people.

4.3 Close on a Positive Note

The closing reflects the mastery of our dawah technique. Some people have polished introductions, but their presentations are too long, so they lose people when they are trying to invite them to the deen. When and how to close takes many years to learn, and we must close on a positive note. Those who have been working in dawah have keys. We must connect with them and learn these keys.

Remember, a kind word can encourage a depressed or lost person. It can be a lifeline for a person drowning in sorrow when they receive a little bit of your attention. In these days and times, compassion is probably the most valuable gift many people can receive.

CHAPTER 5

THE SOCIAL WORK

5.1 Spiritually Connect People with Their Lord

ONE DAY, A YOUNG MAN lost his keys, and he told me about it. I told him, "I can tell you how to find them."

"Really?" he said.

I said, "Yes, but this won't work if you don't believe."

He said, "Okay, tell me."

I said, "Ina-lillahi wa-Inna elayhe rajiun (Surely we are from Allah and to Allah, we return)."

He said this, and he went back to his apartment to look for his keys. Well, about an hour later he came walking up the street saying aloud Allah Akbar because he found them. By the way, this was a Jewish young man. Now, where he learned this Allah Akbar I never knew, but I know I never taught it to him.

We, as inviters to Allah, have to learn how to teach people even small things that will connect them with their Lord. For example:

1. SubhanAllah (Glorified is Allah),
2. Masha-Allah (it is by Allah's will), and

3. In-sha-Allah (if Allah wills it).

Once, I knew a renowned professor from a university in America. He told me that when he was in World War II he was stationed in Algeria. He told me he knew a little boy who taught him something that he never forgot. He said the boy told him when you want to do something to say Insha Allah. We never know how what we do or say today might affect others today or tomorrow. We must always be careful to remember this with reverence for Allah and with fear for what actions our decisions might send forward for the people we meet.

5.2 Taleem (Teachings) Daily in the Field

There are many different ta'leems to have while you are in the field inviting people to Allah. First, the inviter needs to take some time and read to himself, maybe tafsir (explanation) of verses of Qur'an or Hadith. Then he should go out of this ta'leem refreshed, trying to implement what he learned. It's all about teaching and learning. There should be some time of the day when you have some tea or coffee in your area. There should be time devoted to teaching the new shahadas (converts). Then, there is teaching those who want to learn Arabic.

I once had a non-Muslim student who was learning Arabic with me in a downtown local coffee shop, which we called our headquarters. I used some techniques not only to teach my students, but also to engage the crowd. Sometimes, you can read something about history. Others will hear and might join in. We also have what we call ricochet teaching, which is when you have someone else read to you, and you ask questions that other people may have wanted to ask. It helps people maintain interest and demonstrates an understanding of the needs of your audience.

5.3 When Should You Have Ta'leems

We should try to have our teaching sessions daily at the same time. After lunch is a good time, that is after 1 p.m. Also, in the morning is good at about 10 a.m. We also found an afternoon session at about 3 p.m. is very fruitful. These are times of the day when you can find people both available and interested in a change of topic from their daily routine. While not all of these times are good for some people, most people will find one or more of these times convenient.

5.4 Smile

If we smile, others will smile with us. Sometimes all a person needs is a smile and a kind word. People are looking for genuine smiles. The whole world is frowning, angry and in a hurry. Be peaceful, happy, smile, and move at your own pace. You will be amazed at the results.

5.5 The Inner Smile

When are you satisfied with Allah, the Lord of the Worlds, and He is satisfied with you, you develop a deep inner radiating peaceful smile that comes from the soul. People can see it and feel it. It attracts others.

5.6 Be Sensitive

A sensitive person is one who is quick to show or feel the effect of a force or the presence of something. The inviter to Allah must show delicate feelings or judgments. People are easily offended. When you are dealing with people, you are dealing with secret spiritual issues, so you must be sensitive.

5.7 Relax Others

This worldly life has people uptight and busy with their hustle and bustle. If we want to reach people with truth, we must be relaxed and help others to relax. What often relaxes people is to engage them about familiar and positive things. For each one of these dawah points that we are talking about, there are thousands of different doors to enter through and a thousand different exits. One entry that I have found most pure is to engage a person with an open, honest heart. I mean, you talk to them without an agenda other than to help them if you can, or to enjoy an honest conversation with them. Most often, if they do need help, it seems Allah sends just the right words to open the problem for mutual examination and to offer medicine that begins the healing process. Most of the time, in these situations, I later marvel over the conversation because it doesn't even sound like something I would typically have thought to say.

5.8 Listen with Your Heart

Often we talk to people, and people speak to us, but are we listening with our hearts? The Qur'an was revealed to the Prophet Muhammad ﷺ in his heart; then, he acted on it. People want you to hear them with your heart; to feel and taste what they are saying. When the hearts communicate and understand one another, each party receives a release of personal anxiety, which opens up their spiritual blockages and allows them to gain some spiritual knowledge. People must be opened up before you begin to place spiritual jewels within them. This is a process that doesn't happen overnight.

5.9 While Someone Else is Speaking, Make Dua for Them Silently

It isn't what we say that often influences people. It's what we don't say that moves them. Often when people are talking, we should silently pray for them because it's not our beautiful words that will move them, but it is the guidance from above, from the Almighty, that will guide them. We must always stay connected with Allah. This connection, if it is true, will help facilitate change in others long after we are gone. We will reap the benefits of these flowing blessings from Allah. Sincere prayer changes things.

CHAPTER 6

WISDOMS

6.1 Keep an Open Heart and Mind

AS INVITERS TO ALLAH, WE must keep an open heart and mind so that we can continuously receive guidance from Allah.

There are four types of guidance:

- First is the guidance of instinct. This is with a child from the time of its birth. It feels a need for food and it cries in search of it.
- Second is the guidance of the five senses. These two types of guidance from Allah, the first and the second, are found in both humans and animals. It is stronger in animals than the human being because the human being develops these in stages.
- Third is the guidance of the intellect. The human being was created to live with others, so just having these first two types of guidance alone wouldn't be enough. He must have a sound mind to correct the mistakes of the senses. Haven't we seen that a sick

person thinks something bitter is sweet, and some people see a straight piece of wood in the ocean as if it is crooked? Allah told us,

As for Thamud, we guided them, but they loved blindness over guidance.—Qur'an 41:17

This is an example of guidance of the intellect that was rejected.

- Fourth is the guidance of religion and legislated laws. This guidance is a must for those whose desires have overcome the intellect, whose souls have been made a servant to their lustful desires and for those who have taken the path of evil and sin and have become an enemy to other human beings. When injustice has taken place between people, this type of guidance will help those who are wrong to see the need to curb their desires because their desires have taken over their intellect. With this type of guidance and regulations, it will become apparent to men so they won't exceed limits ordained by Allah.

These limits are there because there is so much we don't understand or even have real experience with that can, nevertheless, affect our lives. These limits give us guidance to navigate things within and outside our understanding, whether we are aware of them or not. Good examples were when people believed eating pork was no problem, then we began to find out how many diseases and illnesses could come from eating pork. To this day, we have no way of knowing if we have discovered all the adverse effects pork can have. Another was when we did not realize we should not worship or pray to anyone other than Allah (The Creator). Other examples we think of as more spiritual, such as Allah Himself, the angels, and heaven and hell, but our knowledge of them is so limited that we are reticent to describe them in any detail. Even though we know some things about these concepts, we do not know how to interact with or navigate these places and things. The laws we have protect us from our ignorance in dealing with these things. This is the fourth type of guidance.

As inviters to Allah, we must search for guidance from Allah. Ask Him continuously for His help and ask Him to make us victorious over our desires and passions after having worked hard to the best of our ability to know Islamic laws. We must stay humble and continuously ask and search for Allah's guidance. We should never look down on others. We shouldn't think that we are saved. We should never believe that we have it all figured out. Be humble servants of Allah with our hearts and minds, continually searching for guidance in all our deeds and actions.

6.2 Knowledge

We must know Allah and His Prophet Muhammad ﷺ. We should have the proper knowledge of tawheed (monotheism) and act upon it. Knowledge should increase our humility. If it's making us more arrogant, we must check ourselves.

The more you know, the more you realize that you don't know. Learn to say, "I don't know." Don't learn to say, "I know." If you say, "I don't know," then you can be taught until one day you will know. If you learn to say, "I know," you will be asked until you say, "I don't know."

6.3 Action Based on Knowledge

Our actions, as inviters to Allah, should be based on sound knowledge, which is the knowledge of the Qur'an and

Sunnah. To have intellectual information is one thing but to have knowledge which you act upon that gives you experience, is something that opens the doors to wisdom and understanding. We have become great intellectuals, but what is our legacy that we have acted upon and established? The Qur'an was revealed to be followed.

6.4 Reach Out and Help Someone

We must remember someone reached out and helped us. So, we must reach out and help someone else. If you want to polish yourself, sincerely help someone else. It's a feeling that you can't explain. It's like a natural high.

6.5 Talk to People on the Level They Are On

Ali Ibn Abi Talib—may Allah be pleased with him—once said,

> *Speak to people on their level of understanding. Do you want them to consider Allah and His Messenger Muhammad liars?—May Allah be Pleased with him.—The Hadith*

The one who calls to Allah must learn to speak with people based on their level of understanding not based on the inviter's knowledge. At times we are so filled with ourselves we are unable to diagnose a person spiritually. Consequently, we give them medicine, but it's not what they need. We haven't reached them on their level. Listen with your heart, not your ears. Feel with your bones and see with your skin.

6.6 Keep Yourself in the Spirit of a Student

When Prophet Moses (Musa) was asked, "Who is the wisest in the land?" He said, "I am." So Allah told him to go down to where the rivers part, and there Musa would meet another of Allah's servants, Khidr—and the story goes on in Surah Al-Kahf in the Qur'an.

However, Musa couldn't follow Khidr because Allah hadn't given him the knowledge and wisdom to behave as a student with one who was sent to teach him. I was once told that when the student is ready, the teacher will appear. Giving dawah, we must maintain the spirit of a student who is eager to learn, and Allah will teach us.

6.7 Think Five Times Before You Say Something and You Might Be Right

It was said by the Messenger of Allah ﷺ,

> *Whoever is silent has been saved.—The Hadith*

He ﷺ also said,

> *Whoever wants to be safe, he must be silent.—The Hadith*

He ﷺ also warned us about the harm of the tongue when he said,

> *A Muslim is one who other Muslims are safe from harm by his tongue and his hands.—Sahih Bukhari, Volume 1, Book 2, Number 9*

Also,

> *Shouldn't I inform you of the easiest of worships which is also easy for the body? Silence and good manners.—The Hadith*

Waheed ibn al-Ward said, "Wisdom consists of ten parts. Nine of those parts come from silence, and the tenth is being isolated from people."

It was said by the Messenger of Allah, "Whoever believes in Allah and the Last Day, say something good or be quiet."

The Messenger of Allah said, "The excellent character of a person is to leave things that are not his business."

The Messenger of Allah once said, "The first one to enter this door will be a man of paradise." So, Abdullah ibn Salaam entered the door. People began to gather around him and told him what the Prophet said. They asked him what he had been doing? He replied, "I am weak, but I have a peaceful breast, and I stay away from things that don't concern me."

One day a man passed by Luqman—may Allah have mercy on him—at this time, Luqman had a lot of people with him, and asked him, "Aren't you a slave from such and such tribe?"

He replied, "Yes."

The man asked, "Didn't you used to be a shepherd in such and such mountains?"

He replied, "Yes."

The man asked, "How did you obtain this status that I see you with now?"

Luqman said, "By speaking the truth, and having long periods of silence about things that don't concern me."

The tongue is one member of the body that can do great harm. But it can also benefit us if we use it correctly. The Prophet Muhammad ﷺ warned his nation in numerous hadith about the injustices of the tongue. He advised us not to argue because people of the past were led astray through argumentation.

He further advised us not to curse anyone. He even went as far to say that the one who cursed others is not a believer.

Without careful management and training, our tongues can cause us much trouble. However, it can also be a reason that we are rewarded by Allah. We find that the Prophet, ﷺ often said that a good word is charity.

O you who are inviters to Allah, be careful of what you say. Speak good or be silent. Remember, actions speak louder than words. Say good, positive things to people. Encourage people to do good. Race to do good. Work hard, talk less.

6.8 Meditate on Allah's Words and Ponder Over the Creation

The inviter to Allah should ponder over Allah's words often. Just as the rain from the heavens brings out the vegetation from the Earth, the words of Allah bring life, iman (faith), to the heart, which gives the believer a precious, marvelous, fulfilling life. If the inviter has no sign of life, how can he pass it out to someone else? Allah asks the question,

> *Are they not pondering over the Qur'an or are their hearts sealed?*—Qur'an 47:24

Also, in the creation of the heavens and the earth, the night and the day are signs from Allah for those who ponder over them. When the inviter to Allah points people to Allah's signs in creation, hopefully, it will encourage them to think about their Creator, Allah.

6.9 Sit with Others and Enjoy Silence

It was said by a pious man that wisdom consists of ten parts: nine of these are in silence, one part is in isolating yourself from people.

Once, we went to visit a pious man in Jerusalem. His name was Shaykh Hussain. They said he was from the family of the Prophet ﷺ and that he lived in a room behind and under Masjid As Sakhra. When we visited him, he gave us zaatar with olive oil, bread, and tea. I took a friend of mine with me. We stayed for about 45 minutes eating and drinking in silence. The shaykh never spoke to us. He was busy remembering Allah.

My friend asked me, "When is the shaykh going to drop something on us?"

I said, "He already did." I told him, "He's been dropping something on us since we entered. You just didn't hear it."

There was a young boy named Sami who used to serve this old man. I asked the boy once, "What does Shaykh Hussain do at night?"

The boy told me that he doesn't do anything. "He just stays up all night, remembering Allah," and he said, "I'm up with him remembering Allah."

Another time before we visited the same shaykh, I found a group of people sitting with him for more than an hour. They were offered tea, bread, zaatar, and olive oil through sign language. They sat there with the old man eating, drinking, and talking to him. Not once in that hour did I hear him respond to them verbally. It takes time for hearts to communicate. Silence can help facilitate this.

6.10 Be Spiritually Conscious at All Times

From Allah we come and we will return to Him. Often, we become very comfortable within our zones. We become complacent, satisfied within ourselves. Beware! Usually, this is when Allah will send a test or a sign. We have to be spiritually conscious to see these signs. Often, it's very subtle, and it comes within the blink of an eye. Some tests we pass, but often we fail, and we aren't spiritually conscious enough to know we are being tested. The person giving dawah is continuously being tested. These tests from Allah help us grow spiritually.

One day, we were downtown behind a mailbox. We had three Qur'ans open. One was in English, another was in Arabic, and we had an Arabic tafsir book opened. A man appeared out of nowhere, very well-groomed, and said to us, "As Salamu Alaykum, keep reading the Qur'an." We looked at each other, and when we looked in the direction in which he was going; he disappeared. Oh inviter to Allah, remember Allah and give salutations on the Messenger of Allah ﷺ often.

CHAPTER 7

ADVICE TO DA'EES

7.1 Be Natural

BE YOURSELF AND ACCEPT WHO you are. Who are you? You are a righteous Muslim. We shouldn't try to be Malcolm X, Imam Siraj Wahhaj, Shaykh Hamza Yusuf, etc. We should be ourselves. Learn to develop yourself based on who you are and your level of understanding. There is always room for us to grow organically; Islamically. When we act naturally and don't try to put on a front, we are laying the foundation to see how Allah is molding us. There was a song that said, "The whole world is a stage, and everyone is playing a part. The stage is set, and the scene is a broken heart." (Fantastic Four, 1966)

Allah created everything on the fitra (the natural order of things). People are searching to meet genuine people that are honest and sincere. These are qualities that should be apparent in us from practicing Islam. The inviter to Allah should act naturally, not artificially, or superficially.

I asked a university professor whom I had known for many years, "What do you do spiritually for your soul?"

He said, "I go to the woods where there is peace and quiet and enjoy nature."

I told him that there was a time in my life when I couldn't have understood him, but now I do. "You are tired of man-made religions and phony people so, you go to the woods to appreciate nature in its natural form, which the Creator created. And this is a fitting, spiritual experience for your soul according to your understanding."

7.2 Find Out What Interests a Person and Enter That Door

One of the easiest ways to get to someone's heart is to enter through something that they like. We have found in the past that the Christian missionaries studied how we, the Muslims, give dawah, and they incorporated it into their Christian dawah. There is a Christian minister in downtown Chicago right now who studied us for years. Now he's using our methods of giving dawah, and he's become famous and successful. The Muslims stopped giving dawah, and he picked up our techniques. So he's inviting people to falsehood and getting results. Christians take care of their religious missionaries. They don't have to worry about food, clothing, shelter, or their children's education.

Unfortunately, Muslims mock their ministers, and they don't give them anything but a hard way to go. I think the reason for this is that we, as Muslims, no longer value inviting others to the truth. We are too chained to the dunya (worldly life). We have forgotten that our primary job in life is to worship our Lord and invite humanity to the truth. So we are blocking the door and stopping people from coming into Islam. But, our Lord, Allah, is in charge of dawah.

We have found so many renowned Islamic organizations who weren't out giving dawah daily, and they refused to provide the daily workers any Islamic materials which they had stored up in their closets collecting dust. Some of them even lied and said that they didn't have any Islamic fliers.

7.3 Respect Everyone, Even the Bum

Respect everyone. If you want to be respected, then respect others. What goes around, comes around. The inviter to Allah must have a high level of respect towards others, especially when he knows each person is a servant of Allah, whether he is aware of it or not. Every diamond in the rough needs to be polished. Only a diamond can cut another diamond. The bum that we look down on may be a precious stone in the rough. Allah has to train us before we can see this. Each diamond must be cut differently to bring the light and brilliance out of it.

The Prophet ﷺ once frowned and turned away from a blind man, Abdullah ibn Umm Maktoom, who came to him while he was preaching to the chiefs of Quraysh. Allah corrected this action in the Qur'an where it is enshrined as an example of incorrect behavior (we are all human) for all time.

As inviters to Allah, we must not assume that we know who should be given dawah. We must give this invitation to Islam to all human beings. Why are we disturbed when a bum comes up to us and asks us for a quarter? Maybe Allah is sending him to us for another reason. Do we spend more time trying to give a particular race or class of people dawah rather than dealing with the poor and downtrodden? Is our deen really for Allah or do we have ulterior motives to feed our egos?

7.4 Learn to Flow

And the herbs (or stars) and trees both prostrate themselves (to Allah).—Ar-Rahman 55:6

When the stars appear and the trees bear fruit, they are prostrating to Allah, moving within their natural flow. We must learn how to flow. We have to stop being artificial. A good inviter to Allah must learn how to flow with all circumstances and conditions. We shouldn't force our ideas and influences on others. Be natural and flow, and things will take their natural course which Allah has ordained.

There was a man who used to pass by us downtown and would curse me out daily. As long as he was cursing at me, I knew he was okay. One day, while some Muslim brothers were visiting me downtown where we were giving dawah, this same man passed by me and started cursing at me. Those brothers wanted to jump on him and beat him up. I told them, "He's a local and he's fine as long as he is cursing me out. When he stops doing that, I'll worry about him." Many years later, I found out that he was from Armenia, and many of his family members were killed by Turkish Muslims and that's why he was so bitter towards Islam.

7.5 A Spiritual Operation

A spiritual operation can last three to five seconds. It can be done with a smile, a hand wave or a kind gesture. As inviters, we must learn to be skillful surgeons because we are operating on hearts, not bodies. Remember, the angels operated on the Prophet ﷺ to remove the blemish which Satan put in his heart. Just as one must be a skilled surgeon to operate on a patient, you must be a skilled inviter to perform spiritual surgery on someone's heart.

7.6 Recognize Good Qualities in Others

We should recognize good qualities in others and point them out. Everyone wants to be known as someone special.

Since most of us are always complaining about the bad qualities in others, why not recognize their good qualities? We have been told by our Beloved Prophet Muhammad ﷺ,

> "Whoever believes in Allah and the Last Day, let him say something good or be quiet."—Sahih Bukhari, Vol. 8, Book 76, Hadith 482

You help people do good by recognizing that they do have some good qualities and that there is hope for them to increase in positive ways, which will affect their future activities. Everyone needs confidence and recognition. Kind words go a long way.

7.7 Remember the Book of Allah is Our Guidance

The Messenger of Allah ﷺ said that Allah's Book, the Qur'an, is Allah's rope stretched out from the heavens to the earth. It was reported in Muslim's sound hadith from Zaid ibn Arqam—may Allah be satisfied with him,

> One day the Messenger of Allah ﷺ stood up amongst us to speak to us and he had some unclean water. This place was between Makkah and Madinah. He praised Allah—glorified is He. He began to warn us and remind us. He said, 'Oh mankind, I am only a man (human being). It is imminent that a messenger will come from my Lord (an angel), and I will answer him. Surely I have left amongst you two weighty things. The first is the Book of Allah. In it is guidance and light. Then take the Book of Allah and hold onto it.' He encouraged them to do this. Then he said, 'and also al-Bait (the people of my family). I remind you by Allah about the people of my family.—The Hadith

It was reported by Muslim that Umar Ibn Al-Khattab—may Allah be satisfied with him—said that the Prophet of Allah ﷺ said,

> "Surely Allah elevates some people with this Book, and He disgraces others."—The Hadith

Ibn Abbas reported—may Allah be satisfied with him—that

> A person who doesn't have the Qur'an within himself is like a dilapidated building.—The Hadith

It was reported by an inviter to Allah that one day, while giving dawah in the downtown area of a western city, an intoxicated man suddenly approached him. The person giving dawah began to read Surah Al-Baqarah. The drunken man tried to hit the person giving dawah but could not. He tried again but could not. He tried a third time but he could not hit him. It was as if Allah had formed a shield around him that could not be penetrated. The drunken man started crying and cursing the Muslim giving dawah and left. One week later, the same drunk man was seen in the masjid sober, dressed in clean clothes, praying with the Muslims. Allah guided the drunken man and made him a Muslim. Often, we don't realize how powerful the Qur'an is and how just hearing it affects people.

There was also a story of a Muslim brother who was standing on the street corner giving dawah when somebody got off a bus that was going in another direction. He walked up to the Muslim and asked him, "What are you saying? I was riding on a downtown bus, and I got off so you could tell me what you were saying because I could feel it when we rode by." The Muslim brother giving dawah didn't even realize that he had been saying a verse from the Qur'an over and over again for the past hour. Surely Allah has power over everything.

Once, there was a drunk bum who walked up to a Muslim brother. The brother started reading the Qur'an to him in Arabic. The bum said, "That sounds like a hit record!" Then, after a few minutes, he said, "Turn me loose!" The next day, the bum was sober, wearing a brand new suit and asked to hear that hit record from the day before again. The Book of Allah is our Guidance.

7.8 Live the Sunnah (What the Prophet Did, Said, and Established), Don't Talk It

There was a sound hadith in Ibn Maja where it was reported by Yahyah Ibn Abi AlMuta, who said he heard Irbad Ibn Sariya saying,

> *"The messenger of Allah ﷺ stood up amongst us one day and gave us an excellent sermon. It affected us so much that our hearts became fearful. Tears flowed from our eyes. Some said, "Oh Messenger of Allah, surely you have given us a power-packed sermon. Give us advice on what we should do so we won't forget." Then he said, "You must fear Allah (have taqwa). Hear and obey your leader even if he is an Ethiopian slave. You will witness, after I leave you, severe controversy. So, hold on to my sunnah and the sunnah of the rightly guided khalifas (rulers; Abu Bakr, Umar, Uthman, and Ali). Hold on to it with your teeth. I warn you against new things in this deen (innovations). Every innovation is an error."*—At-Tirmidhi, Book 1, Hadith 22

This hadith tells us to fear Allah; that is, we should do what has been ordered and leave what has been forbidden by Allah and His Messenger. Then, he said to hear and obey your leaders even if its an Ethiopian slave. After that, the Messenger of Allah ﷺ warned us about a fitna (a trial of faith or practice) coming after his death between the Muslims.

> *So, if you understand what I said to you about this fitna between the Muslims after my death, and you would like my advice to you during this time, then I say to you hold firm to my Sunnah. Also, hold firm to the sunnah of my khalifas—the rightly guided ones—whom Allah guided to the straight path.*

At the end of this hadith, the Messenger of Allah warns us against innovation in the religion. Innovation will lead us astray, and everything that leads us astray is in the Hell-Fire.

The inviter to Allah must be busy living the Sunnah, not just talking about it. Let people see us as real Muslims following our beloved Prophet Muhammad ﷺ staying away from fornication and adultery, not drinking alcohol, using drugs, selling drugs, etc. Let our lives be our testimony. Actions speak louder than words. The manners of the Messenger of Allah ﷺ were established by the Qur'an. We must exemplify excellent manners, openly and secretly. Be kind, show others love, respect, and be conscious of others' needs.

7.9 Pray for the Sick

Inviter to Allah, visit the sick, you will find Allah there. Ask them to pray for you and you should pray for them. We have physical and spiritual illnesses. A lot of physical diseases are related to spiritual ailments. Just as we need physical doctors who can attend to us when we are physically sick, we also need some spiritual doctors who know how to address spiritual illnesses. Sick people need someone to spend time with them. They need to be around positivity. We must encourage them to think positively about the Creator. We must know that, regardless of our circumstances and conditions, Allah is in charge. Surah Al-Fatihah heals. Try it. We know that it works.

Remember that everyone has a soul which Allah has created. As inviters to Allah, we must remember that every person is exceptional because Allah has given each one of them a soul, and their soul will return to Him. Regardless of a person's condition, we should want what's best for every soul. We should want every soul to be guided with the light of Allah. There are many spiritual valleys in this life. Allah has placed us where He has ordained us to be. We must pray for others even if we can't reach them physically or spiritually. Remember, Allah can reach and touch anyone at any time in any circumstances.

We shouldn't give up hope on any soul; everything is possible with the help of Allah. People need real love and concern. If they are unable to listen and heed the signs that Allah sends them, then the All-Knowing (AlAlim), the Caretaker (Rabb), the Creator (Al Khaliq), will teach them in His way. Allah has more than 99 names or attributes. These are just three. Think good of others and pray for them: this may help them to change their lives. Souls need food just like bodies need food. However, to understand precisely what kind of food a soul needs for nourishment is a wisdom that only Allah can give. Every soul needs to be fed in stages. Our Lord develops us in degrees and phases according to our ability to comprehend His signs and guidance.

7.10 Start When Others Stop

Say: 'Oh ibadi (My slaves) who have transgressed against themselves (by committing evil deeds and sins)! Despair

> *not of the Mercy of Allah. Verily, Allah forgives all sins. Truly He is Oft-Forgiving, Most Merciful.* —Qur'an 39:53

Inviters to Allah should hope the best for other human beings. When a person is in a bad spiritual state, that is, using drugs, drinking alcohol, etc., we shouldn't give up on them. When they have given up on themselves, we should start with them, hoping that Allah will guide them and have mercy upon them. We used to take people to a detox center before we could work with them and teach them Islam. Remember, there is hope for every soul. In the 1960s, the masjid was the detox center. I had a friend who kicked a heroin habit by becoming Muslim, staying close with his Muslim brothers and continually going to the mosque.

7.11 Always Be in Motion Even if You Are Standing Still

> *Whatsoever is in the Heavens and whatsoever is on the Earth glorifies Allah, the King (of everything), the Holy-One, the Almighty, the All-Wise.* —Qur'an 39:53

The trees, rocks, mountains, and all of creation are moving constantly, praising Allah. If an inviter to Allah isn't moving externally, he should be moving internally, always praising Allah with his heart and tongue. We must have good thoughts in our minds and hearts about others, even if they are doing bad things. We must lead others to what is right and not force them. The old people used to say, "You can catch more flies with honey than with vinegar." We must always try to keep positive thoughts in our hearts and minds.

7.12 Be Lively

People tend to like being around others who are lively. We should have a cheerful spirit towards other human beings. When they come in our presence, they should feel alive, not dead. For this to happen, our hearts have to be focused on Allah, the Almighty. When people see us, they should remember Allah. They should have good thoughts. It should make them want to do good. If we are spiritually lively, people will feel light and have a good, clean feeling in our presence. They will be able to feel and taste iman (faith), although they won't know what it is. We should be light on others, not heavy.

7.13 Children Love Attention, and So Do Adults

It was reported that the Messenger of Allah ﷺ used to play with his grandchildren, Hassan and Hussein. It is well-known that children strive for attention. They want to be noticed; they want you to play with them, talk to them, read to them. They need your time and attention, which will help them grow and develop naturally. Adults love attention too. They need someone to listen and talk to them.

In giving dawah, we must learn how to use these natural inclinations to draw and invite people to Islam. We should be friendly with children as well as adults and say things like, "Oh, that's a nice hat," or, "Oh, that's a nice coat."

7.14 Be Light on Others Not Heavy

> *And by the mercy of Allah, you dealt with them gently. And had you, [Muhammad], been severe and harsh hearted, they would have broken away from you; so pass over [their faults], and ask [Allah's] forgiveness for them, and consult them in the affairs. Then, when you have made a decision,*

put your trust in Allah. Certainly, Allah loves those who put their trust [in Him].—Qur'an 3:159

Oh, callers to Allah, learn how to be gentle with people. We shouldn't be harsh when giving dawah. We must learn to overlook the faults of others and ask Allah to forgive them. You can catch more bees with honey than you can with vinegar. Gentleness doesn't necessarily mean weakness. We should be strong internally with iman but gentle in our speech and mannerisms when giving dawah, which is all the time. We must learn to build an internal tolerance to deal with people from all walks of life. Allah will teach us this if we are sincere in our dawah efforts. Fear Allah, and He will guide you.

7.15 Be Servants

We have been told by our beloved Prophet Muhammad ﷺ,

"Be slave servants of Allah and brothers to one another."— *Sahih Muslim, Book 32, Hadith 6216*

So, first and foremost, we have been ordered to worship Allah and be His servants. To be His servants, we have to know Him and know what He has commanded us to do.

We should also be servants to humanity. They said that any slave girl could take the Prophet's hand in Madinah and take him anywhere with her to assist her. If we are going to be excellent inviters to Allah, we must learn how to serve humanity. We should practice helping people solve their problems, whether it's drug abuse, alcoholism, child molestation, prostitution, etc. People are spiritually sick, and we have the cures for those sicknesses and diseases: Islam. Being humble servants of Allah, and servants to humanity, we should be able to listen humanely. When we pay attention, we will see these illnesses and be able to lead these people in the right direction. Then they can begin to get physical as well as spiritual help to combat their problems. Islam is the solution, and it works. So we must become active and use the tools we have to get proper results.

7.16 Be Peacemakers

We often say, "Oh Allah, You are As-Salaam (the One to whom all peace belongs) and from You is all peace, blessed are You, Possessor of Majesty, and Honor." So, we recognize that to Allah belongs all peace because He is al-Salaam. Inviters to Allah, be peacemakers.

We should be spreading peace.

With Allah, make your peace through obedience and submission. It's rewarding and a continuous challenge.

Find serenity within yourself, which is also often challenging but best facilitated through obedience to Allah.

Encourage goodwill between other human beings.

Wish peace upon the Muslims.

Say words of peace to whoever follows right guidance.

Make peace with your parents, elders, teachers, stepparents, fellow workers, children, siblings, cousins, friends, and neighbors.

Our job is to spread peace. If there is no peace, there is no happiness. Stop holding grudges against others. Learn to forgive and forget. We must be peacemakers on earth. Everyone is looking for peace in their lives. The peace that Allah gives a believer cannot be explained in words. I remember when I first became Muslim in 1969 when someone would say as-Salamu Alaykum (May Allah's peace be upon you), the hairs on my body would stand up, and it made me feel lovingly elated. One salam would suffice me for that whole day.

7.17 Avoid HellRaisers

Oh you who believe, fear Allah and be with those who are truthful. We would like to say many of these dawah points were recorded before. We were blessed to give some dawah classes in Madinah al-Munawarah in a dawah office under Baqia and some dawah classes in Toronto with the Canadian dawah Association. The book that these writings were in was lost, and the only things remaining from them were tapes which we had recorded in Madinah. We became very frustrated, and we were unable to reproduce these dawah points until a student in Madinah, who is like my son, asked me to travel with him to Riyadh to meet some people to talk about dawah. Subhanallah, those 100 dawah points came back in one night with an additional 80 points. Many of these points are based on 50 years of experience, actually working in the field of dawah.

As callers to Allah, we shouldn't have confrontations. If people are intoxicated, we shouldn't spend much time talking to them, but rather, we should pray for them. We should try to avoid arguments. Once, I can remember we were giving dawah on a bridge on the campus of Michigan State University where there were some Christian missionaries about 50 feet from us calling listeners to Christianity. They were telling people that they were going to hell if they didn't believe this or that (their Christian doctrine). Sometimes they would say bad things about the Prophet Muhammad ﷺ and they would say aloud that Islam was the devil's religion. We never addressed them. We just kept selling and giving away incense and giving dawah.

After some time, non-Muslim students would come to me and say, "We hate those people, why are they so offensive and arrogant? Why can't they be like you: quiet, nice and reserved?"

We would tell them, "Do not be angry at them. They think that they are doing what is right. They have been taught to act like this. Pray for them and forgive them, and thank Allah that you are not like them. Keep an open heart and mind."

Sometimes, when you're giving dawah, people will come up just to argue with you. They want to draw a crowd so they can prove their point. If people aren't listening to us, why do we continue to talk? Sometimes the best thing to do is to say a kind word, smile and give a person something to read and tell them to get back to you. We must remember: action speaks louder than words.

Another time in Chicago, a man came up to us talking loudly and saying that Muhammad was a liar. We just read about fifty verses of Surah Al Baqara and left him to argue with himself. Many people are dealing with spiritual forces, and you are not talking to them. Instead, you are talking to their jinns (beings created from smokeless fire whose existence is different from that of men), and their jinns are talking to you. Remember, gentleness and kindness are the keys. Avoid hell-raisers and mischief-makers. Try to look for people searching for the truth, who are truthful and honest. dawah requires true love, time, and patience.

7.18 Be Concerned About Others

The Messenger of Allah ﷺ was very concerned about his uncle Abu Talib who protected him his whole life. Allah revealed a verse that says,

> *Surely you cannot guide those who you love, but Allah guides whom he pleases.* —Qur'an 28:56

As da'ee, we must be genuinely concerned about other human beings' welfare. People can feel whether you are worried about their physical, spiritual or mental well-being, or if you are just trying to force your religion on them.

Many of us came into Islam, and we had the wrong understanding. We left our parents and relatives behind, and we spent all of our time with other Muslims. Some people even began to hate their parents and relatives. We might hate some of their religious beliefs that contain setting up partners with the Creator, but we must love them and respect them because they are our parents who gave birth to us. They raised us to the best of their abilities and cared for us when we couldn't care for ourselves.

We should also keep our ties with relatives. Remember, they knew us when we weren't so religious. Many of us were the ones leading them into doing bad things. We shouldn't look down on people as if we are better than them. It's just Allah's mercy that He guided us. Our parents should be foremost in our lives, so we should talk with them only when we do so with respect and dignity.

Once, there was a drug addict who used to visit us in our downtown office for dawah. When he came, we always used to try to say positive, good things about him. He used to look around in amazement as if he knew we couldn't be talking to him, and he couldn't believe we were saying positive things about him. His look was as if he was saying to himself, "Who the hell are they talking about?" After some years, this person became Muslim and told us that his mother never talked positively to him. He said he never got the love and concern from his family that he got from us.

7.19 Visit the Sick

Visiting the sick reminds us that health and sickness are all part of Allah's qadar (ordinance). Muslims should try to visit the sick as often as possible. If we live in Muslim countries, we should visit the sick in their homes, as well as in the hospital. Try to bring them a gift. They will appreciate whatever we give them. What is meaningful is that we thought of them, not only the gesture of giving. We should ask them to pray for our families and us. Just your presence will make them happy and feel better. If you give them candy or some sweets (if they don't have diabetes) it would make them feel loved and cared for. Sometimes we offer them Zamzam water and some simple books or fliers. If they are Muslims in a non-Muslim society or hospital, leave that Muslim patient some leaflets and sweets so they can give dawah to the doctors, nurses, visitors and fellow patients.

We had a Muslim brother, Sulieman, in a hospital nursing home in East Orange, New Jersey. We always used to leave him incense, oils, and dawah material. Although he couldn't walk, he was still giving dawah to the nurses, doctors, visitors, and other patients. When you visited him, your iman would be increased by the time you left. He loved to talk about Islam, Allah and our beloved Prophet Muhammad ﷺ. When he came to Madinah, Saudi Arabia, often, he couldn't leave his hotel room. We used to visit him and have beautiful ta'leems together. We miss our brother Bashir SuleIman so much. May Allah's mercy be upon him and grant him Paradise, Ameen.

When you visit sick people, they don't have to be Muslims. Listen to the sick when they are speaking to you. If you are wise, you will find that Allah is with them. If you visit non-Muslims, just ask them what happened to them and say "May Allah heal you." They will ask you questions. Don't worry about talking about religion. Just your presence will open conversations. Be patient, kind, and considerate. You will be surprised by what Allah allows people to see.

7.20 Visit the Graves

Visiting the graves will remind us of death. This keeps us humble. As inviters to Allah, we must realize that Allah has given each human being a soul and that every soul will return to its Lord, Allah, and it will have to be accountable in front of its Lord on the Day of Judgment. Visiting the graves will increase our fear and reverence for our Lord. It will also teach us to respect every human being. It will remind us that from Allah we came, and to Allah we shall all return. May Allah guide humanity to His Guidance (Islam) Ameen. He who Allah guides cannot be led astray, and he who Allah allows to go wrong, no one can guide him. The pen is raised and the ink is dry. Everything has been created with an ordinance.

7.21 Make Tawheed Foremost and Alive in Our Daily Lives

As Muslims, we are naturally inclined to be inviters to Allah. Our connection with Allah must be strong. Surely sometimes, we may fall weak, but we must get up and keep striving. Surely our works will be judged according to the seal of our actions. The sound mind must strive to obtain knowledge for the pleasure of Allah. With sincerity, Allah may bless that sound mind with al ma'rifa (certain knowledge of Allah). Further growth may be rewarded with the tawheed (worshiping only one God, the Creator) of good works (doing everything we do because it will please Allah, with no other reason for doing anything). Allah is Merciful. Are we merciful? Allah is Gentle. Are we gentle?

We must know that Allah sees us at all times because He is the All-Seeing and the All-Knowing. So, we must be careful how we treat Allah's servants, whether they consciously know that they are servants of Allah or not. We must treat other human beings with the utmost respect, even if they don't respect themselves. Our actions, based upon Allah's tawheed (unity), should bring out the best qualities in other human beings.

7.22 Reflect on One Verse at a Time

Allah said,

> *Then do they not reflect upon the Qur'ān, or are there locks upon [their] hearts?*—Qur'an 47:24

Pondering on verses will unseal our hearts. Yes, our hearts have become sealed, sick from repeatedly sinning willingly or unwillingly, knowingly or unknowingly. Pondering will lift these seals. We are now talking about something you cannot see because we are talking about the spiritual world. The inviters need seals to be lifted from their hearts, and Allah's light will eventually be reflected through them and be a catalyst in helping remove other people's seals. Islam is transmitted from heart to heart.

CHAPTER 8

MORE ADVICE TO DA'EES

8.1 Always be Willing to Share

This quality is crucial for the inviter to Allah because when it is impossible to reach a person through conversation, you can share tea, coffee, or a donut with them. Even if you don't talk in the beginning, be a good listener. If you listen sincerely to others, they will listen to you.

It is better to give than receive. We must share our time, sympathy, concern, and human feelings with others. People are dying for someone to share with them emotionally. They are looking for a listening ear, a sincere heart, and a silent tongue. Our beloved Prophet Muhammad ﷺ and his companions always shared with others. The Ansar (the people of Madinah that welcomed the Muslims who migrated to Madinah) shared what they had with the Muhajireen (the Muslims who migrated to Madinah). Share a smile, a kind word, a minute of silence, a piece of candy, a wave, a handshake, a hug, a tear, a laugh, etc.

8.2 Remember, Steel is Put in Fire to Make it Strong

Allah forges our will, spirit, and iman (faith) by testing us. The test is the fire that tempers our spirit. The more Allah loves you, the more He tries you. Allah tested our beloved Prophet Muhammad ﷺ. His own family and people rejected him and persecuted him and his followers, but this only strengthened their iman (faith).

When we accepted Islam, our immediate families were our most significant test. Still, they were only used by Allah as a means of purifying us and making our faith like steel, durable and invincible, trusting solely on Allah. Inviters to Allah must withstand criticism and adversity. Surely in bitterness, there is a unique sweetness, only to be explained by the taster. The sweetness of iman felt by the heart is difficult to express by the tongue. Keep striving, working hard, and inviting humanity to Allah.

8.3 Always Remember Allah in All Circumstances and Conditions

This practice is essential for the caller to Allah to keep foremost in his heart and mind. Tests never stop coming. The harder you work in the way of Allah, the more severe the tests become. You will be sent beautiful women, money, jobs, anything to keep you away from inviting humanity to Islam. Allah reminds us in Suratul Baqarah, verse 152, that if we remember Him, He will also remember us.

One of our greatest weapons, which will protect us from seen and unseen evils, is the remembrance of Allah. Happy or sad, remember Allah. Rich or poor, remember Allah. Whether you have troubles or no troubles, remember Allah. Encourage others to remember Allah often.

It is common for a Muslim to say al hamdulillah (all praise is due to Allah) in every circumstance and condition. Our job as da'ee is to introduce people to their Lord, Allah. They have been disconnected from Him for such a long time. The greatest gift that Allah can give a person is the knowledge and awareness of Himself. From Allah we come and to Him we will return. Nothing happens without His permission. Keep your tongue moist with the remembrance of Allah and the heart burning, branding His remembrance in it.

Once, we knew a beautiful inviter to Allah in Chicago. He was very high spirited. He used to give dawah every day. His wife would come to him in the field midday daily, asking for money. That brother was on fire, an inspiration, but eventually, his spirit was killed, and he stopped giving dawah.

8.4 Remember, What Seems to be Far is Near

Remember, inviter to Allah, that everything coming is near, even Paradise and the Hell-Fire are near to us although they seem to be far away. I can remember when I was 20 years old in 1971. Now, that which appeared to be far is knocking on my door.

We shouldn't be fixed on seeing the success of our dawah efforts in our lifetime. If we are sincere with Allah and our Lord accepts our dawah, it will produce fruits in Allah's time, not in our time. Remember, we have been told not to say bad things about time because Allah is time. I can remember older people telling young people, "If you don't understand what I'm telling you, father time will teach you."

Remember, the Qur'an was sent by Allah from the Preserved Tablet in the heavens by Jibril on the heart of our beloved Prophet Muhammad ﷺ. Allah has preserved His Word (the Qur'an), which isn't a creation. He will take it back to Himself in the Last Days. We must know and believe what Allah has promised us, that surely the believers will be successful. O caller, work humbly with confidence and assurance that the Lord of the Worlds is watching you, and He will accept the work of the righteous.

8.5 Follow Your First Mind

We have been told by our beloved Prophet Muhammad ﷺ

> *Be aware of the intuition of the believer, surely he sees with the light of Allah.*

Inviter to Allah, never negate the intuition of your first mind. Be aware of it. You can't explain it, but if, at the time, you just feel something isn't right about a thing, then stay away from it. Allah guides us and sends us help in mysterious ways.

8.6 Don't Use Others, Help Them

Sometimes people have the spirit of using others, spending their time and energy and not helping them. As inviters to Allah, we must be generous and giving. We must give our time, effort and wealth in helping other human beings. I didn't say Muslims only. We must be ready to help all the children of Adam. Our beloved Prophet ﷺ told us,

> *Allah helps the servant as the servant helps his brother.—At-Tirmidhi, Vol. 4, Book 1, Hadith 1930*

Some people just need kind words, a sincere hug or a listening ear. Others need a watchful eye. Some people need some tea or a cup of coffee or a meal. A homeless person just needs a place to stay. A drug addict needs a program. We must understand the nature of people, understand their needs, and help them in a righteous way. Allah will bring them to Islam in His time.

We must have sincere concern for other human beings. We should try to help them improve their lives. If we do this with sincerity, they will inquire about Islam. People are in pain spiritually, physically, and mentally. They need help even though many of them don't even know it. Some souls are sick while other souls are dead. We must help as well as pray for others. People need heart to heart talks, walks and sincere listening sessions.

In this day and time, it's hard for people to trust others. We must strive to be truthful and trustworthy. Our word must be our bond, and our bond must be life. We should be ready to give our lives before allowing our words to fail.

8.7 Don't Be So Critical

As an inviter to Allah, we should not be inclined to find faults in others or to be quick to judge.

As people come to us with spiritual sickness, we must ask Allah to help us ask the right questions. A doctor can't treat an illness until he examines the patient and diagnoses the illness. How can we treat a person spiritually when we haven't examined that person? This takes time. It is not easy to do in one sitting. After the spiritual sickness is understood, the medicine can be given. The wrong prescription can prove to be fatal. A little spiritual medicine at a time should be administered. Allah will guide you in this manner. Overdoses can kill.

Give people a chance to look at themselves. If they see themselves, they will want to change. Instead of always criticizing a person, find something about them that they can be complimented on.

8.8 Be Thankful if You are Well

It was said by Isa (Jesus), the son of Mary,

There are two kinds of people in the world. Some are sick and some are well. Be kind to the sick, and thank Allah for your health.

If we are thankful to Allah, He will increase us. As inviters to Allah, we must not look at others in terms of what they have been given and marvel over it, wishing to have it. We must be thankful to Allah for what He has given us. We have Islam, which is the greatest favor Allah bestows on a human being. If we have been chosen as a torch-bearer of the truth, an ambassador of the Lord of the Worlds, representing His beloved Messenger, Muhammed ﷺ, then we must be grateful.

To be in good health, have a sound mind, have use of our faculties, be able to see and talk—wow, what a blessing from the Creator! Shouldn't we be thankful? Remember, as inviters to Allah, our job is to try to connect humanity with the Lord of all the Worlds. The best remembrance is the remembrance of Allah and the best dua is "all praise is due to Allah." The remembrance of Allah is more valuable than the world and all that is in it. Give praise to Allah and teach others to praise Him always.

8.9 Let People in Your Front Door, Don't Let Them Enter Through the Back Door

Do not enter people's homes through the back door. Instead, we should knock and go in from the front door. We also know that Satan likes to distract people from doing good works.

When I was living in Norfolk, Virginia, I had a Muslim friend who I used to visit in the hood often. I noticed that as we were talking about Islam, he always got knocks on his back door. I told him, "Don't open that door, tell them to come around to the front door." Well, most of these people refused to come around and knock on the front door. It was Satan coming through the back door. As Muslims, as we are striving to live a righteous life, we must stop being slick-undercover, as if we are doing something wrong. This is the most righteous work we can do. Always enter through the front door.

Be righteous and enter through the front door. Do the right thing. Stop trying to always get over on others. Those who are slick will only be tricked.

8.10 Spiritually Clean Your Own House

We are often advising others to clean themselves up spiritually, but what are we doing behind closed doors? We can't invite others to do good and neglect ourselves. We must spiritually clean our own house first then, we can begin talking to others. We must become living examples through our actions, not our conversations.

I remember after being overseas for many years, my mother, who was a Christian, told me that she patronized a store in Staten Island, New York and that the people who owned the store were Muslims. She told me, "When you come to New York, I'm going to introduce you to these people." When I visited her several years ago in the summer, she took me to that store. I was dressed at that time with a kufi and thobe (robe).

When she introduced me to these people, the first question they asked me was, "Are you Muslim?"

I glanced around the store and responded, "Are you Muslim?" because they were selling pork and alcohol. Then, I asked them if they prayed five times a day.

They looked at me as if they saw a ghost. They said, "No."

I said to them, "The real question you have to ask yourself is, are *you* a Muslim?" I told them, "Yes, I'm Muslim, and this is my mother, who is Christian, and you are preventing her from coming to Islam." Before leaving their store, I said, "May Allah guide and help you."

8.11 Understand the Apparent So We Can Learn the Implied

When studying the explanation of the Qur'an (tafseer), you will find that many of the Scholars of the Qur'an explain the apparent meaning of some verses and also explain the implied meaning as well. Their in-depth study of the Qur'an and its Arabic grammar, along with their teachers who can trace *their* teachers back to the Prophet ﷺ has led them to understand both the apparent and the subtle meanings. In life, the propogator of Islam must study the evident implications of situations that are presented to them thoroughly so they can understand the implied meanings. For example, a man walks up to you while you are giving dawah and starts to curse you out. The apparent meaning is that he is crazy; however, if you are looking into the implied nature of the situation, he is probably a person who needs attention. He needs some love, someone with whom to talk.

Look at the Columbine shootings. We, as a society, were unable to understand the apparent signs of the shooters before it happened. We couldn't see that these youths were in crisis. They were implying that they needed attention. We missed the apparent and the less evident signs because of our spiritual blindness by this worldly life and our greedy desires.

We must reach out to touch others positively. Anyone has the potential to change their lives for the better. People are sick spiritually. They are screaming, crying, making all sorts of noise and we can't even hear them. Now governments are falling, and leaders are being discarded because we do not understand the apparent; therefore, how can we expect to be given the subtle knowledge of the implied by the Almighty Creator, Allah?

8.12 We Should Look to be Trained, Not Look for Fame

Every discipline in life requires some specialized training. If we want to become skillful in something, we must first be educated in that field. After that, we must work in that field under supervision to obtain experience and, finally mature as practitioners in our discipline.

However, beware of fame. After all these steps have been taken, recognition will come to you and try to knock you off your saddle. If you entertain fame, it will dethrone you and impede your progress for growth and progression in your field. Recognition carries a spirit with it which is designed to alter the very nature of the human being. Everyone sort of loves it; however, it inflames the ego—one of our many enemies—and stops our spiritual growth.

Today, you will find many people in leadership positions that have not been adequately trained. As a result, the essence or substance of the knowledge of those particular fields is becoming extinct. It is also a sign that we are living in the last days.

Once, I was in a downtown area giving dawah, observing some Muslim brothers trying to give out some copies of Qur'an in English. As I watched them, it was clear to me that they had not been skillfully trained in what they were doing. It took me less than five minutes to see this. So I went down the street, called one of the leaders of an Islamic dawah organization, and asked him to come with me because I wanted to show him something. When he arrived, we went up the block together. As we stood and watched what these people were doing, I asked him if he knew them.

He said, "Oh yeah, these are our old workers. They are our teachers and elders in this work."

I was speechless because I brought him up the street to show him that these people needed to be appropriately trained in giving dawah. They were chasing after people, making their invitation appear to be cheap and of no value. I realized that many leaders themselves have become self-proclaimed. The grassroots experts haven't trained them. Therefore, the right knowledge of the art and skill of this spiritual profession, dawah, is becoming extinct. I took a young brother from the group and tried to train him, but he was too distracted in the downtown area to grasp the transmission. I think the transfer of this knowledge is so simple and subtle that most people can't see it and understand it.

Once, there was a shaykh from Saudi Arabia in Canada giving lectures at a mosque. I told my three sons, who were giving dawah with me daily in downtown Toronto, that I would like the shaykh to come with us one day and give dawah. After a few days, we saw the same shaykh at a downtown Islamic Center while we were praying the afternoon prayer. I told him that we were giving dawah and that we would like him to help us. He said, "Give me ten minutes, and I will go with you."

I waited for him and sent my sons on their posts while I took the shaykh with me to one of the downtown corners. As I started dealing with the people, I noticed that the shaykh was lost. He had a lot of theoretical knowledge of Islam, but he didn't know where to begin in dealing with the ordinary people on the street.

It was clear he had been given information, but he wasn't trained in the application of the knowledge. After fifteen minutes, I suggested to him, "Shaykh, I know you're busy, and I don't want to hold you up but thank you for coming out with us. Your presence has inspired us." I was honest; we were happy to have him with us. Although we were in Toronto for several months giving dawah, we weren't able to find anyone willing to learn from what we knew.

8.13 Fight Your Own Nafs

Surely the nafs (self) is prone to do evil except the one upon which Allah has bestowed His mercy. Those who prohibit their egos from their desires, Paradise is their return. If our nafs is not checked, how can we help to lead others? We will become a hindrance, blocking others from guidance. If we have girlfriends, how can we encourage others to see the pitfalls of fornication and adultery? If we are smoking, drinking alcohol, and using drugs; how can we help others stay away from those vices of the devil?

We should suppress ourselves from going towards disobedience and stay away from Islamically forbidden things that feed the craving of human desires. We must stay away from the self that tries to seek pleasure through unlawful means. We Muslims must fulfill our desires by lawful means, like marriage and being responsible.

Some people—Muslims—used to say, "We smoke marijuana because it's natural, it calms the nerves and it helps us to think better when we read the Qur'an." Note that the restricted laws of Islam are our success. All intoxicants are forbidden in Islam. If we are weak, we shouldn't try to justify our wrongdoing. Admit that we are weak and ask Allah to remove this overwhelming compulsion to do wrong; ask Him to guide us to do right. Never accept the behavior as right and always strive to leave the behavior for something better.

8.14 Let Allah Mold You

And mention in The Book (The Qur'an), [Oh Muhammad], the [story of] Maryam (Mary), when she withdrew in seclusion from her family to a place facing east. She placed a screen (to screen herself) from them. Then, We sent to her Our Ruh (Angel Jabril, Gabriel), and he appeared before her in the form of a man in all respects. She said, 'Verily, I seek refuge with the Most Gracious (Allah) from you if you do fear Him.' The Angel said, 'I am only a messenger from your Lord [to announce] to you the gift of a righteous son.' She said, 'How can I have a son when no man has touched me, nor am I unchaste?' He said, 'So [it will be]. Your Lord said, 'That is easy for Me and [We wish] to appoint him as a sign to mankind and a mercy from Us (Allah), and it is a matter [already] decreed (by Allah).—Qur'an 19:16-21

Maryam was molded by Allah. He prepared her at a young age before He gave her His mission. As inviters to Allah, we must be aware that we have to submit to Allah; let Him mold us. He will send people to us to help prepare us for giving dawah. We must be diligently working on whatever level Allah has us on. He will raise us in degrees. When the student is ready, the teacher will appear. We must learn to take instructions, not give them. Allah offers important keys when we least expect it. In the breasts of the freedmen, lies the graveyard of secrets.

CHAPTER 9

REAL STORIES FROM THE FIELD

9.1 A Physical Touch Can Be a Deep Spiritual Touch

There was a good Muslim brother who used to visit many of the drug addicts in his neighborhood. When he would visit, he knew they were sick, strung out. From time to time, he would give them a light massage and tell them, "Don't worry, you are going to be alright in the future. Allah is going to bless you." Many of these same people are practicing Muslims now. Physical touch is one thing, a mental touch is another, but this brother wanted to touch their souls.

9.2 Get Out of the Way and Let the Hearts Talk to One Another

Once, I was reading a tafseer of the Qur'an to one of my teachers in Madinah. Often, I would read to him, but he wouldn't talk to me to give me feedback. One day, when I was coming from his class, I started talking to myself, "Why do you keep going to this class, and this old man hardly talks to you and explains things?" Then, I said to myself, "You understand more from him not talking than you understand from those shuyookh who are always talking." We have to grow past the self which is blocking our path to spiritual growth and let our hearts communicate with other hearts.

9.3 Reach Inward—Study Your Own History and Try to Get to Know Yourself

Many people travel through life and never get to know themselves.

There was a young man who used to say bad things about his father. I got tired of him complaining so I told him, "I'm tired of hearing your mother talking through you." I asked him, "When was the last time you saw your father and spent time with him? Then tell me what you think about your father, not what your mother thinks."

The boy became angry with me. However, he did visit his father and spent time with him. They became close and shared mutual love between themselves. This incident opened up a door that had been locked in my own life. I realized that my grandmother was teaching me to hate my mother. When I revealed this to my mother, she sat down and asked me with a puzzled face, "How did you know that?"

Do we know ourselves and understand our own historical experiences? Here we will find many locked doors. However, the keys are there. Through dawah and understanding others, we can unlock doors within ourselves that have been locked for years if not centuries passed down from our ancestors.

9.4 Recognize the Spirit That We Are Dealing With

We are so often overwhelmed by the physical we forget people have souls. These souls belong to their Creator. When we are dealing with others, we shouldn't be focused on the outer appearance; instead, we have to be thinking about the spirit. Spirits often come to us through others; people are only the vessels. The elders used to say about some people, "That's an old soul."

One day, a man and his wife got into an argument, and then the wife got mad and walked away. Her husband got mad and followed her around the corner. When he touched her on the shoulder, she turned around, and it wasn't her but another woman. So he went back to the place of the argument, remembering Allah, and his real wife returned. Spirits change forms in the blink of an eye. In giving dawah, we must learn to understand the spirit that we are dealing with, not so much the individual person.

9.5 Tie Your Affairs to Salah

In order for us to be successful in giving dawah, we must tie all of our affairs to salah. We should make our plans and strategies around salah. Salah will help you distinguish between right and wrong, good and bad.

I remember one day, as we were giving dawah, a man walked up to us with a big Bible in his hand. We said to him, "Hey, what's going on?"

He told us he was disappointed because he was supposed to meet someone, but they never showed up. We told him not to worry. Maybe something happened to the guy. He then asked us if he could spend some time with us. It was actually time for our salah. We told him we had to go down the street to a restaurant. So he came with us. We went in and made wudu in the bathroom. (We shouldn't make wudu in public restrooms unless we tidy up after ourselves. We must give good dawah and clean up behind ourselves.) When we came out of the bathroom, this man was still waiting for us. We told him it was time to make our prayer.

He said, "Can I come?"

We told him, "Yes." We then went across the street in the grass behind a building with our prayer rugs. We said, "Excuse us, we have to pray." We faced the Qibla, did our takbir, and completed our Dhuhr salah. When we finished, the man was gone. So, we went back to our post, giving dawah.

Twenty minutes later, the same man walked up to us and said, "What did God tell you when you were praying?" He said that when *he* was praying, God told him so and so. Well, the truth came to us about this situation.

We told him, "You are a liar. Stop lying on God. When you came to us, you were lying, you weren't supposed to meet someone, you just used that to start a conversation with us, and now you want to lie and tell us God told you something." We said, "You call yourself religious, but now you're lying on God. Now you want to talk about God." When we mentioned this, he ran away.

> *And remember when Ibrahim said, 'Oh my Lord! Make this city (Makkah) one of peace and security, and keep my sons and me away from worshipping idols. Oh, my Lord! They have indeed led astray many among humanity. But, whosoever follows me he certainly is of me. And whoso disobeys me still, You are indeed Oft-Forgiving, Most Merciful. Oh, our Lord! I have made some of my offspring to dwell in an uncultivatable valley by Your Sacred House (the Kabah in Makkah) in order, Oh Lord, that they may perform As-salah (Iqamat-as-salah), so fill some hearts among men with love towards them, and provide them with fruits so that they may give thanks.—Qur'an 14:35-37*

Ibrahim left his offspring in a valley with nothing so that they may perform salah. Today when you see Makkah, everything is present there. It shows us that if you establish salah, everything that is needed will come.

One day, Abdulrashid and I were having ta'leem in his building on Chidester Place in Ypsilanti, Michigan, in a public room. We said that we would have ta'leem once a week, even if nobody showed. We started reading the tafseer of Surah Al-Baqarah about when Ibrahim raised the foundation for Allah's House, the Kabah, in Makkah. I said to Abdulrashid that we need to lay down a foundation like Ibrahim.

Abdulrashid said, "I know how to build a foundation, but we don't have any money."

I said, "Insha Allah, we'll get the money." At the time, we owned 20 acres of land in West Ann Arbor. So we raised money from ourselves, the Qur'an students, children and a few other believers. We bought wood, and we laid a foundation for Allah's house on our land.

A non-Muslim passed by and said, "I can show you how to build the walls." So I, Abdulrashid, the children from the Qur'anic school, and the non-Muslim built the walls, and we put a roof on top of it. Then we laid some carpet in it. We finished around Asr salah. It took us a week to complete it.

As soon as we finished it, a Jamaat from out of town came and said, "We heard you were building a mosque." So we prayed Asr salah in it. You could feel goosebumps coming up on you when you prayed in it.

We went home and came back the next day only to find that the mosque had been burnt to the ground. The children, as well as the adults, cried like babies. They asked us why anyone would want to do such an evil deed. One said, "I guess the mosque was too pure for this world, so Allah took it back to Himself."

9.6 Practice Timing–Time Management

We have been told by our Beloved Prophet ﷺ "Don't curse the time, Allah is time." Without Allah, there wouldn't be time. We, as Muslims, are taught about the importance of time in our salawat (prayers).

We must pray five prayers within their proper times. Each prayer comes in at a particular time and ends at a specific time. When giving dawah, we must have a schedule. What time will we start daily? First, give your time to Allah. Make two rakaat (divisions of prayer), read a few surahs from the Qur'an, make dua for Allah's help and guidance, then go out and give dawah. Establish coffee breaks. Never be too busy to stop and treat someone to coffee or a sandwich and listen to their problems. Remember, your time should be used in pleasing Allah. Be a servant to humanity. Have a regular time for ta'leem daily in the field. Even if nobody is there, read as if a thousand people are listening. Be sincere in deed and intention.

I can remember, while giving dawah, different people would come up to me and ask for help. I would give each person an appointed time later that afternoon or early that evening to meet me. During the day, as Muslims that knew me came to greet me, I would ask them to give me sadaqah (charity), which I would collect and give to those people when they came to their appointments. If no one gave me sadaqah, I would give from myself. Last of all, I would borrow the money from someone and pay them later.

A friend in need is a friend indeed. As callers to Allah, we must learn how to befriend people in time. There are many degrees of friendship. There are friends we work with whom we have working, friendly relationships. There are friends we have as students with whom we study. There are friends we have as neighbors with whom we have neighborly relations. Some friends are relatives with whom we have family relationships. But there are usually very few friends with whom we share our intimate, personal, religious friendship.

9.7 Remember: Light Has Many Different Degrees and Stages

Allah is the light of the heavens and earth. He is the Guide for the heavens and earth. He guides people with His light. He is the One who illuminates the heavens and earth. He illuminates the heavens with His angels. He enlightens the earth with the prophets, the scholars and the believers. It was said that Allah beautified the earth with trees and vegetation. Light consists of four parts:

1. The light which manifests in the eyes and can be seen as the light of the sun, etc.
2. The light of seeing—This light makes things seen by the eyes. This light is more noble than the first one.
3. The light of the mind—This light makes subtle things understandable, which have been hidden in the darkness of ignorance, for those who can see. He will ascertain something and see it.
4. The light of the truth—This light makes apparent subtle things that didn't exist in your realm of understanding, but existed within the Kingdom of Allah. This light will allow something to be present and seen that was unknown because it existed within Allah's knowledge and had not been revealed. The knowledge of Allah cannot be changed. So, seeing something is only seeing its existence. The light of Allah's light is the Qur'an. It's an explanation for all of the knowledge brought by all of the prophets from Adam to Muhammad—may Allah forever be pleased with them, Ameen.

I can recall, before I became Muslim, I once brought an English Holy Qur'an translated by Maulana Muhammad Ali.

I can remember trying to read it in English. I couldn't complete reading one page at a time. I would fall asleep before finishing the page. It was too much light. It overloaded my circuits. I couldn't hold this much light, so I tried not to force myself with prolonged readings. I was in the womb trying to understand the light of the Qur'an, and I hadn't even been born yet spiritually.

When the Prophet ﷺ made the ascension with the angel Jibril and they reached the seventh heaven—arriving at the Lote Tree—Jibril couldn't go any further as it was too much light. He knew his limitations. The Messenger went on to meet Allah and see Him, but he had to be prepared for this twice. Once when he was a child, the angels came and opened up his chest, washed his heart with Zamzam water and filled it with wisdom.

As da'ees inviting people to Islam, we have to work within the light of our understanding. In time, Allah will increase our capacity to take in more light and, in turn, give out much of that light which we have received soothingly, meaning it is blessed (has barakah) but not in a piercing way.

Remember, regardless of how high you ascend spiritually, you must descend back to where you originated from, and be able to deal with the ordinary people. Why is it that, in many cases, when we seem to be spiritually intoxicated, we can't deal with everyday people? We want to deal with the so-called intellectual elites. In many cases, we have artificial spiritual growth and not natural spiritual growth. The natural spiritual growth is when the mind, body and soul grows spiritually, and develops naturally through real=life experiences. Artificial spiritual growth is when we have simply accumulated information, and we become top-heavy, having minimal expertise. We obtain wisdom with a limited amount of soul searching. Our remembrance of Allah must be continuously strong and constant, never wavering although faith increases and decreases.

If a person wants to grow and develop in his or her field fully, they must first establish a strong foundation in that field through study and practice under the tutelage of a well-experienced teacher. In this case, the student will grow in stages and degrees. As we grow in our knowledge, wisdom, and understanding in these fields, unseen doors (opportunities) will open up, and only by the permission of the Almighty will we be able to enter these doors, benefit and ascend to the next level.

My original teacher for giving dawah was Abdullah Nafis. He is the one who turned me on to selling and giving dawah. We started in Queens, New York. He used to be known as Brother Alfonso 6X from Temple #7B Corona, on Northern Blvd. He used to sell one thousand newspapers per week. He was well-known in the community in the 1960s as one of the top paper sellers in Temple #7. He learned from Brother Mather and Brother Skelsis. I worked with Abdullah Nafis in the early '70s. He taught me until I became skillful and began selling a thousand papers per week. By Allah's mercy, I sold one thousand newspapers per week for seven years.

I was also blessed to study with other teachers. Brother Patrick from Harlem was another teacher of mine. Brother Leonard taught him. Brother Patrick, who was later known as Brother Musallah, was as smooth as a diplomat. Abdullah Nafis' technique was fast and cunning while Musallah was slow, deliberate, and smooth as silk. He was like butter. I worked on each teacher's method until I mastered it. Then, after that, I developed my natural techniques in time.

We developed a crew of ten brothers, each one selling a thousand papers a week. We were selling ten thousand newspapers a week in New York City when the Nation of Islam changed leadership after Mr. Muhammad died. We then took shahada with his son, Imam Warith Deen Muhammad, may Allah have mercy on him. We continued selling and giving dawah up to 1979 when I went to Makkah to study Arabic and Islamic studies.

9.8 Let Allah Wash Our Hearts; We Can't Do It

When Muslims pray five times a day, through it, Allah washes our hearts. One prayer is equal to ten prayers, and so five prayers are equal to fifty prayers. Our beloved Prophet ﷺ was first ordered to make fifty prayers every day, and as the report goes, he met Musa (Moses), who told him to go back and ask Allah for a reduction. If you want to know more about this, read about the ascension of Prophet Muhammad ﷺ.

The Creator Allah is looking at our hearts not our bodies. So we should submit to Allah willingly and allow Him to purify or wash our hearts. He can also do it unwillingly, as He does whatever He pleases. He is the Irresistible One above His servants.

Let your heart be washed in salah (prayer). Focus on Allah, cut off your worldly ties, and give your heart totally to Allah. Let Allah wash your heart, as you give indiscriminately, inviting humanity to Allah while having no malice or hatred towards other human beings. Let Allah wash your heart as you read His Word, the Qur'an.

> *Those who spend in good times, as well as during hardship, they hold their anger and pardon all men. Allah loves al-muhsineen (the doers of good).* —Qur'an 3:134)

Allah's trying us is only a means of purification. We must never look down on any human being. Remember, they are souls just like we are. I remember there was a man who was a wino. He was drunk every day. I would always be kind to him. There was another brother who used to be mean and harsh with him. One day, we were in the mosque, and a young man with light on his face, cleanly dressed, stopped us and gave us salaams. He said to my friend, do you remember me, I was that wino who you used to be harsh with, now I'm Muslim. Then he said to me, "Thank you, brother, for always showing me love."

9.9 Be Balanced

Allah said,

> *"Thus we have made you, (true) Muslims (believers of Islamic Monotheism and true followers of Prophet Muhammad), a just, balanced nation, that you will be a witness over mankind, and the messenger Muhammad will be a witness over you."*—Qur'an 2:143

I can remember when I called myself Muslim in the '60s. We were very unbalanced people. We believed that the white man was the devil. When we were asked if all white people were the devils, we responded, "Yes, even the babies."

Once, my father found a sword under my bed in his house. He said, "If Elijah Muhammad asked you to kill me, would you do it?" I never answered him. So he told me, "It's time to pack your bags and leave my house," and I left. We had extreme ideas. We were new Muslims, and we believed in what we were taught in the Nation of Islam without question. We didn't know that our leader and teacher, Mr. Muhammad, knew very little about many aspects of Islam. We were blind followers. Thanks to Allah, He spared us from our ignorance. After Mr. Muhammad died, I took allegiance with his son, Imam Warith Deen Muhammad. He gave us shahada after we had been Muslim for seven years.

Now, I must tell the truth, although we had many strange teachings that were designed to make us love ourselves and our people, I benefited from the discipline and many of the Islamic teachings of that time in the Nation of Islam. And our brotherhood of Islam was powerful. We stopped celebrating all Christian holidays. We stopped drinking, smoking, and partying. Fornication and adultery were forbidden. We were taught that the restrictive law of Islam was our success. If you were caught breaking any of these laws, you were put out of the temple for 90 days. We followed instructions to a tee. When we gave salaams to one another, it gave us new life. Some of us ate once a day, once every two days, or once every three days. We were super disciplined.

My first trip to Hajj in 1977 was paid for by Muhammad Ali, the former heavyweight champion of the world and Jabber Muhammad, his manager, who was also one of Mr. Elijah Muhammad's sons—may Allah have mercy on them. There, I realized that we didn't know as much Islam as I thought we did. Even our Islamic leaders needed translators.

The Nation of Islam developed many qualities that could benefit the Muslims in the East. The Muslims in the East have preserved many of the sciences of Islam. These would benefit many Muslims in the West.

In the Nation of Islam in the old days, the Muslims had the zeal and spirit of Islam. In the East, the Muslims seem to be lacking that zeal and conviction today. Their enthusiasm seems to be more about their culture than Islam. We need knowledge, eagerness, spirit, and action. This is the straight path (sirat al-mustaqeem).

We were once speaking to some learned scholars in Madinah. We told them that, "All praise is due to Allah that He has blessed you all to preserve the knowledge of many of the sciences of Islam, but we have been given something that you lost, although we had very little knowledge of Islam. We have been given the sincerity and the spirit, fire and, zeal of Islam." When we asked them what would happen if the body of knowledge and the sincerity, zeal and spirit of Islam came together, they bore witness that it would be a living soul: complete Islam.

If you have a brother or sister in Islam who seems to have extreme ideas as new Muslims, don't shun them. If they are sincere, Allah will show them their mistakes and guide them to develop and have a balanced life. Believe you me, I know this from experience. Islam is a beautiful, balanced way of life that has everything in it to help us to be complete, kind and loving human beings.

I saw a video on YouTube called *My Brother, the Islamist*, which was about a man whose brother was very extreme in his ideas. In this case, he needs to give time to let his brother grow. He is only acting on the knowledge that has been given to him, and he sincerely believes it. If you want to be in the know, study Islam, not your brother. You may be given insight that he doesn't have. Whoever makes Islam a burden on himself, he will be destroyed by it. We must learn in stages and degrees. If you study people, you will find that most extremists don't even know their religion, regardless of what that religion is.

Remember, a child learns and grows in degrees and stages. Many of us are products of our environment. You must crawl before you learn to walk. Remember, baby talk doesn't make much sense. Babies make a lot of noise and they are forever crying. It is the same with new spiritual babies. Remember, changing diapers is the responsibility of the person in charge of these babies. Then comes potty training. The girls usually learn faster than the boys. When people come to Islam as new converts or reverts, they are spiritual babies, even if they don't know it. Unfortunately, we have some grown men leading others in Islam who themselves are spiritual babies. Maturity is displayed by one's character, demeanor, and one's ability to deal with tough situations through knowledge, wisdom, understanding, and enlightenment.

9.10 Look and Listen for Keys Sent to Us by Strangers

And verily, there came our messengers to Ibrahim (Abraham) with glad tidings, they said Salaam (greetings of peace). He answered, Salaam (greetings of peace), and he hastened to entertain them with a roasted calf.

But when he saw their hands went not toward it (the meal), he mistrusted them, and conceived a fear of them. They said, 'Fear not, we have been sent against the people of Lut.'

And his wife was standing (there) and she laughed (either because the messengers did not eat their food or for being glad for the destruction of the people of Lut), but we gave her glad tidings of Ishaq (Isaac) and after Ishaq of Yaqoub (Jacob).—Qur'an 11:69-71

It was said in the explanation of the Qur'an that these messengers sent to Ibrahim were the angels Jibril, Meka'eel and Israfeel. They brought the good news to Sarah that she was going to have a child. Some say they were three angels, some say nine, some say twelve. As inviters to Allah, we must remember that the creation of the heavens and the Earth is indeed a more considerable work than the creation of humankind; yet, most of humanity know not. We must keep our minds and hearts open to receive keys sent to us by strangers. We must not think we have the most knowledge. Allah gives knowledge to whomever he pleases. Look at the story of Musa and Khidr. We may not know who a stranger really is. We must be careful, alert and on guard at all times.

We have often heard it said by old people, "Be aware of how you entertain strangers because they might be angels." We must remember in life that there are many locked doors between us and understanding. Allah has the keys to all doors which He gives to whomever he pleases. As inviters to Allah, we should study the story of Musa, the boy, and Khidr. There was knowledge that Musa (even as a Prophet) didn't have, while Khidr was taught by Allah what Musa didn't know.

One day, a Muslim brother stood in front of a masjid in downtown Atlanta, Georgia inviting people (non-Muslims) upstairs to hear the Friday khutbah (sermon). A very tall man was walking by and was asked to come upstairs.

The man said, "I don't have time, I'm busy."

The Muslim brother asked him again, and he became angry. So the Muslim brother said, "I tell you what, just give me a hug."

The tall, 6'5" non-Muslim man hugged the Muslim brother and said, "That's the best thing that happened to me in ten years. I just finished ten years in prison, and no one there showed me any love."

People are looking for genuine love and concern. Islam offers us the love of Allah, love of His Prophet, ﷺ love for other believers and love and care toward humanity; hoping they will be guided to the truth. People respond to love, not hatred. Of course, we should hate evilness and wickedness in people. However, we must learn how to show the children of Adam love, which will help to bring out better, positive qualities in them.

CHAPTER 10

LANDMARKS, ESTABLISHING YOUR OWN ENVIRONMENT

10.1 Marketplaces

REMEMBER DA'EES, THE MARKETPLACE IS where Shaytan raises his flag early every morning, and he lowers it at night when the market is closing. So we should make dua upon entering the marketplace.

> *There is no deity except Allah. He is One with no partners. To Him belongs the kingdom, and to Him belongs all praise, and He has power over everything and everyone.— Sahih Muslim, Book 35, Hadith 6510*

First of all, you must check out the marketplace. How is the foot traffic flowing? Is there a parking lot near the market? Is there a subway station near the shopping center? Is there a major bus stop in the area? One thing you don't want to do giving dawah is to impede peoples' freedom of movement when they are shopping.

One technique of selling and giving dawah at a marketplace is by moving, walking amongst the people so that you are selling and giving out dawah fliers or books at the same time. Note: Don't stop in front of businesses, people's booths, or stores. You want to be an asset to the shops, not divert customers from them. If you can move to the opposite side from the vendors and not block anyone's business, it is preferable. Now, if you sell something and you are giving them some literature and they happen to tell you what they are looking to buy, you can suggest it and send them to one of the business entrepreneurs. Ask them to tell the vendor that you sent them, and they will look out for you.

You can also work with another Muslim who has a business in the marketplace. Ask him for a small space, and you can give dawah from his business place. You don't want to be arguing with people at the brother's store about religion because you will run people away from his business. So, just give out fliers. Now, if someone wants to talk to you about Islam, invite them to a nearby coffee shop. Also, help the person's store where you are giving dawah. Help him keep it clean and well-stocked. Be a help, not a hindrance. Don't disturb shoppers either. Instead, help them.

10.2 Downtown Areas

We spoke earlier in this book about some types of downtown dawah, but now we will be more specific.

We have what we call 'box selling' or dawah. This is where you stand in the corner of a box in the cement on the sidewalk. You are supposed to master your box. When anyone comes into your box after you have stopped and gotten their attention, you control the situation. In this 'box selling' or dawah, you are never supposed to leave your box; you must master it. This technique is very effective, subtle and extremely powerful, but it takes years of selling with a master and consistently practicing this technique to master box selling or dawah.

You should set yourself up on one of the extreme ends of a box, preferably by the curb or your back against a wall. The beginner should start with his back against the wall because when there is a heavy flow of people, your inexperience won't allow you to see what's happening behind your back. These things I'm explaining to our readers, this is a different world. Allah blessed me to enter this world by being exposed to some of the dawah masters of their time (the 1960s to 1970s) in New York City.

When you stop someone in the middle of your box, don't let them stay there and block the walking traffic, but pull them to the corner of your box where you are standing and deal with them. When we say pull them gently, we mean to lead them gently. It could be with a word or a gesture. Now a proficient master can even stop a person in his box without a word. Just a body movement or a gesture will stop them. Body language is another world. We won't get deep into this science at this time.

Now, box selling or dawah, it shouldn't take you longer than five seconds to make a sale and plant an Islamic seed in the person who has stepped into your box. Your introduction, presentation, and your closing must be smooth, gentle, sharp, deliberate, swift, and to the point—there is no room for guesswork. Your flow, rhythm, and timing must be precise. To be able to do this with precision and understand this technique, you need to sell with a master, and he will continuously point out your mistakes and correct you. Daily, hourly, and even by the second, you'll witness the different scenarios and see how the master approaches them. In time, you will naturally learn and develop. It won't happen overnight. It takes years to learn these things. Brother Lenard and

Patrik (Musallah) were two of the four pioneers of dawah in New York in the 60s.

Now there is a type of selling where you move with the flow of people and sell and give dawah while you're walking. In this type of selling or giving dawah, there is nothing fixed or stationary; instead, you are flowing, moving off of inspiration, stopping people at random. To do this, you must be highly spirited, like a ball of fire. When you touch someone mentally, physically, or spiritually, they are profoundly affected within a split second. This type of dawah is so subtle, it's hard to see it with the naked eye. I taught this dawah to my children, because they were young and full of fire, about to explode. You must be careful with this type of dawah because it is so powerful it can give someone a heart attack.

10.3 Table Dawah Downtown

Now, to give dawah from a table downtown, you should be registered as a non-profit organization. You need two or three Muslim brothers working at a table. Do not encourage people to hang around your table. Make sure you manage people around your temporary "office," so they don't see it as a social hang out spot. They will use your table to attract distractions if you are loose and not careful. As we mentioned earlier in this book, don't stand in the middle of the sidewalk blocking the flow of traffic—respect other people's rights. Don't scream or holler at people. Don't speak loud, trying to draw attention. Be gentle and kind to people. Have a few extra chairs behind the table in case you want to give an old, tired person a seat, or have someone sit and talk to you. Never let anyone block your spot. If it's hot, have some cold water or juice available. If it's cold, have a thermos of hot tea or coffee on hand.

10.4 Universities

When you want to give dawah at universities, you should do it through a Muslim university organization like the MSA (Muslim Student Association). Under this organization, you can set up dawah tables outside the cafeteria area on certain days of the week. You can give ta'leems on campus once a week in a campus room that the organization can get for you. You can invite Muslims and non-Muslims to these ta'leem classes. We used to have lessons at Michigan State University in Lansing, Michigan and Eastern Michigan University in Ypsilanti, Michigan. Many people took shahadas (the profession of faith) from these classes. They were once a week. We always tried to bring new people to these classes. We generally used to teach from two tawheed books: *Kashfa Shubuhat* and *Usul al-Thalatha*. Each lesson was one hour, and at the end, people would ask questions.

Once, we found that the MSA wasn't giving much dawah on campus at the University of Michigan in Ann Arbor. So, we met a Pakistani student and told him that if you set up an Islamic organization on campus, we will teach you how to give dawah. So he set up his organization, and we taught him how to give dawah. Many of the famous athletes began to embrace Islam under this brother.

The MSA approached him and told him that if he merged his organization with theirs, they would make him the president of the MSA. Well, when he joined with them, that put out his fire for giving dawah, and he just blended in with the other Muslims. Unfortunately, some people lose their motivation when others step in. But you can never have too many inviters calling the people to Allah.

10.5 Courthouses

Many people have been giving dawah and selling at courthouses in the West. First of all, people going to court are usually in trouble, they may be facing time in jail, and many of them are open to listening. I used to sell at the courthouse in Chicago, and there was a police officer who used to give me hell for two to three years. Whenever I saw him coming, I would disappear into the revolving door and enter the courthouse. After three years of seeing me and giving me hell, he walked over to me and said, "You must be good at what you are doing, or God must be with you. I have been trying to get you for three years. Keep doing what you are doing, whatever it is."

10.6 Government Buildings

First of all, you don't want to sell right in front of a government building, but maybe you can position yourself on the corner of that government building. You will find many respectable, intelligent people working in these buildings, and they will buy from you and take your Islamic literature. Just be friendly and kind to them. They are human beings, just like anyone else.

10.7 Welfare Centers

These are places where poor people often attend. Welfare centers often have mandatory educational programs for those who receive assistance. So there is an influx of people going in and out of those centers during the month. This is a place where you could easily give out your dawah material.

10.8 Check Cashing Places

You can set up a table a distance from the door of the check-cashing stores. These are places where people have to go to cash their checks. In time, these people will also talk to you and take your dawah material. If you have something to sell, they will also buy from you.

10.9 Supermarkets

This doesn't seem like a good place to sell and give dawah, but it is. In 1977, I used to work selling and giving dawah outside of some supermarkets in Miami, Florida. That is, I gave dawah at supermarkets and parking lots. This was something new for me coming up in New York, but Allah taught me in stages. First of all, I used to hand people a dawah paper on their way in the store and would collect a donation from them on their way out. Those who didn't have their dawah material when they came out, I would go around the supermarket and collect the dawah material that they threw in the garbage.

You can help people with their children. Help older people by opening the supermarket door, and walk them to their cars, or push their wheelchairs. You can also help people put their groceries in their cars. When the people in the supermarket see you doing these good deeds for their customers, they will love having you around their store.

10.10 Motor Vehicles Department

This is the place where you get your driver's license renewed or apply for a new driver's license. In New York City, especially in Queens on Sutphin Blvd, the Motor Vehicles Department used to be packed with people. It was across the street from the courthouses. This was one of our favorite spots for selling and giving dawah in the early 70s. This is one of the places where I was trained by Abdullah Nafis, who used to be called Brother Alfonzo. We used to work this spot from 9 a.m. to 1 p.m. and then would proceed down Jamaica Ave.

10.11 Recreational Parks

We used to "go fishing" in these parks. Meaning we would go out and get people to come to the mosque to hear the teachings of Islam. We were kind of bold and crazy in the late 60s and early 70s. Sometimes we would challenge people in the park, "If we beat you in a game of basketball, you have to go to the mosque with us."

I remember, one day, we rolled up in a park in the hood in Corona, NY, and I was in charge of the mosque's fishing squad that night. So we went into the park to invite those young boys to the mosque, and one of them started fat mouthing us, getting smart. I signaled for the brother who was driving the car to drive up and told the brothers, "Throw that n****r in the car." So, he was thrown into the car, and we then pulled up a bus. Everybody else got on the bus and we took the bus and the car to the mosque. We gave them dinners and a bean pie after the meeting.

Also, on Saturdays and Sundays, people go to parks for picnics with their friends and family. We used to walk through the park selling socks, incense and giving out dawah fliers.

10.12 Festivals

We used to go to the African Festivals selling incense and giving dawah. For the most part, we would sell on the move, or we would set up, burn incense and give out dawah literature. Sometimes, we would take a small part of another person's booth and set up a dawah table, but once we got into the festival, we moved around and sold on our own. You need experience to choose the right spot for doing this.

When giving dawah in malls, many people have set up small shopping carts in these malls, selling incense and oils and giving out Islamic material.

10.13 Door to Door

This is the dawah that can be very rewarding because you enter people's homes and can see how adverse some people's conditions are. In the early stages of my dawah, I sold and gave dawah door to door in Staten Island, Brooklyn, and Manhattan, New York. There was an 85-year-old lady in the projects in S.I.N.Y. who I used to visit every Sunday night. She would read the Bible to me, and I would read the Holy Qur'an to her in English. She used to tell me a lot of stories about slavery down south because her mother was a slave. Well, about 30 years had passed, and one day while I was visiting my mother in Mariners Harbor, Staten Island, I decided to drive past the Mariners Harbor project where I used to hang out years ago. I didn't see anyone I knew, so I kept driving.

I heard a woman scream out, "As-Salaam-Alaikum!" Now, this woman wasn't covered (wearing hijab).

I stopped my car and backed up. I was thinking, "Now, some of your old ways of ignorance and foolishness before Islam are going to pop up."

The lady said again, "As-Salaam-Alaikum! Do you remember me?"

I said, "No, I don't."

She asked, "Do you remember the old lady you used to visit every Sunday in the Markham Homes Projects, Miss Map?"

I got so excited. I said, "Oh, yes. That was my friend, and I loved to sit and listen to her and discuss religion."

The lady asked, "Do you remember that little girl who used to be in the house when you used to visit?"

I said, "Yes, it was her granddaughter."

She said, "That was me. I was listening to your talks, and now I'm Muslim." Her words touched me so deeply, I can't explain how I felt.

Another time, I was at Cobo Hall in Detroit, talking to some brothers. It was during one of Mr. Farrakhan's conventions. All of a sudden, a young Muslim woman walked up to me and gave me the greeting. I returned it. She asked, "Aren't you from New York?"

I became paranoid. I said, "Yes."

She asked, "Staten Island?"

I thought to myself, "You're in trouble." I said, "Yes."

She asked, "Are you from West Brighton?"

I said, "Yes."

She asked, "From Markham Homes Projects?"

I said, "Yes."

She asked, "Did you know Ellsworth and Sheila Mitchell?"

I said, "What? Are you kidding! I worked with Elsworth and did fashion shows with Sheila and Sherry."

She said, "That's my mother and father." She said, "Do you remember those Muslim newspapers my father used to buy from you?"

I said, "Yes."

She said, "They never read those papers, but I was a little girl, and I read every paper you left at our house, and now I'm Muslim."

I was shocked. It took me days to recuperate.

10.14 Social Programs

In the West, they have the African American Month. This is an excellent time to present Islam to people. For example, you can talk about the life of Malcolm X and other social reformers. You could also go to schools with big pictures of the Kabah, Masjid An-Nabawi, a few pictures of Muslims from around the world and just begin to talk about Islam. You can address the people from a universal, cultural perspective.

10.15 Television Programs

It is best to let people who are learned in the deen go on television who know how to answer questions with wisdom. Some people specialize in this field. I believe in staying away from the limelight. There are many public access radio and TV programs, podcasts, etc. where you can present Islamic views. Check your local areas for more information. You can do programs like the history of Jesus, Muhammad, Joseph, Moses, David, Solomon, etc.

10.16 Prisons

It is well-known that Muslims have been giving dawah in the prisons in the West for the last 40 years. Now we have many chaplains working in prisons. If you would like to visit a prison, contact your local Muslim prison chaplain. Muslim prisoners always need kufis, prayer rugs and Qur'ans.

10.17 Drug Abuse Programs

The easiest way to visit a drug abuse program is to know someone who is in the program or approach one of the counselors and tell them that if they have any Muslim clients, they can call you. Tell them you would like to visit them and help out.

10.18 Juvenile Detention Centers

These are usually places that house troubled youth. You can also approach the director or a counselor and tell them you would like to work with them if they get some troubled Muslim youth.

10.19 Detox Centers

This is the entry-level for hardcore drug addicts or alcoholics. They usually sign themselves in these detox centers, and they feed them and allow them to stay there for three days. If you send a person to this center, you have to check on them daily, because they can sign themselves out at any time. If they can last three days, they usually move on to a more extended program.

10.20 Hospital Cafeterias

This is an excellent place to meet people who work in the hospital, but you have to be very discreet in your movement. Have some tea or eat something. Sit and observe the flow of people coming through. You can sit in such a setting reading the Qur'an daily, and someone will eventually come to you and ask a question.

10.21 Outside of Factories

Many people have sold and given dawah outside of factories on people's lunch breaks and when they get off. We used to sell and give dawah in Miami, Florida, at the Longshoremen's Union at 6 a.m. in Overtown.

10.22 Tourists Places

We found that Jerusalem is an excellent spot to give dawah. You will find Muslims, Christians, Jews, and many other people coming there for tourism. People seem open and interested to learn about new things. Just treating these tourists kindly and being genuine with them would be excellent dawah, inviting them to Islam.

We also found that most of the Muslims in Jerusalem are too bitter to give dawah. I can understand that based on seeing their circumstances and conditions, but they are missing out on a bigger picture, the opportunity to invite human beings to Allah. I heard a Muslim in Jerusalem was taking some people on a tour of Masjid al-Aqsa and was so bitter that he was condescendingly talking to the tourists.

If I had to live anywhere else in the world other than Madinah, it would be Jerusalem. The people are some of the most beautiful people I have ever met, like Abu Ramzi and his family, Abu Jawda and his family, Sheik Bassam and his family, and Shaykh Abdul Kareem in Masjid al-Aqsa.

10.23 Bus Stations

Bus stations or terminals are good places for giving dawah. You can meet people from many different nationalities. It is a central location for people traveling to various destinations. In Chicago, I used to sell and give dawah outside of Greyhound and Trailways bus station. You could catch people traveling and also local people working in the area passing by going to and from work, school or lunch.

10.24 Amtrak Train Stations

These are also good places to give dawah, provided the location is in a busy downtown area.

10.25 Flea Markets

This is the place where people come to find a deal, so you can sell and also give out fliers to people who are interested in these flea markets.

CHAPTER II

QUESTIONS AND ANSWERS

Questions & Answers:

How should we give dawah in a downtown area? Should we have a dawah table?

If you want to give dawah in a downtown area, it's wise to register as an organization or a masjid. It's wise to have a license for giving out religious material or selling religious articles and keep your license current. In this manner, you won't have problems with the authorities. Now, if you are traveling and not stationary in a city you are visiting, you can find out if there is an organization or masjid in that city which has a license for giving dawah. We have given dawah in different cities in America without permits. You have to keep moving to do this, and it usually takes experienced, skillful people who know how to maneuver to be successful.

In 1976, when we used to sell in Chicago and give dawah, downtown Chicago was off-limits. Selling and giving dawah downtown was prohibited. So we opened up downtown

Chicago by first selling at the 79th Street and 71st Street Subway Stations, then we worked our way downtown.

Should we use a dawah table downtown?

If you feel comfortable having a table, it's okay. However, you shouldn't be blocking the table and teaching people right in front of it. You should have some chairs next to the table and something to drink also. If it is hot, have some cold juice and water. If it is cold, have a thermos of coffee and tea. If someone wants to talk about Islam, have them sit and give them something to drink. There should be at least two brothers at the table at a time. While one is talking to a guest, the other is watching the table. We should never stand in the middle of the sidewalk, giving out fliers. You must show people respect. Don't force people to take your fliers.

If there are more than two people giving dawah, you shouldn't all be in one place. It'll look like you are ganging up on people. The person in charge should strategically post the people giving dawah, and you must check on them at least every half an hour.

We never gave dawah from tables. We actually rotate the tables ourselves. Sometimes we set up in unique locations, and other times we stayed on the move. It depends on the circumstances and the conditions of your area. Usually, a scout goes to check out the city, and then when his men come into the city, he assigns them their posts.

How was this done?

The person in charge would do this based on his knowledge of dawah. He enters a new city a week before his men enter the city, scouts out the area selling and giving dawah in different locations, testing out which will be the best for dawah. With this experience, he learns critical information like the flow of traffic, when to work, when to take breaks and when to have ta'leem. His job is to guide the men, have daily shura and get their feedback.

To change your post, you must check with the person in charge. He will give you permission. The person in charge must know your whereabouts at all times. Also, the person in charge must be floating, checking on his men. From time to time, he must sell and give dawah with them, motivating them to march forward. Keep your men cheerful.

Also, if the leader of the dawah group leaves to set up in another city, then he must leave someone in charge of that group who must follow that person's orders to a tee. Then, he will call them after he has set up the new city and made all the accommodations needed for his team.

How was this financed?

As for depending on donations to keep your dawah going: we were always self-employed, our dawah never depended on anyone giving us a dime. We generated our own money. After all, we came from the teaching, "Do for self," and, "Up, you mighty nation! You can accomplish what you will." As for our crew, business and dawah were always together. We never separated these two things.

How do you attract people?

First of all, you must learn how to get a person's attention. Within this question, there are many worlds. Explaining this on paper is very difficult, but doing it is like eating apple pie.

First of all, your introduction must be flawless. Certain expressions can be used like "and…", or "but…" which you might mention unexpectedly as if you had a previous conversation with that person and were picking up from where you left off. Other examples are, "and she always looks nice," or, "he is brilliant." At this point, give them what you have to offer like a packet of incense or another item, then close your presentation.

If you're selling something, just say, "it's only a donation for education," or the likes. There was an introduction, then the presentation only lasts as long as it takes to close, and the closing should be in less than 2 to 3 seconds. Now you have planted a seed and performed a spiritual operation if you know what you're doing.

What do you think about giving dawah at train stations?

Well, some of my posts for giving dawah in Queens were the train stations. I used to get up, make Fajr salah, and post up at the train station on 168th Street and Hillside Ave. I was there before the sun came up. I used to pray outside on a piece of cardboard near the train station. Many days I would arrive at the station at about 4 a.m. I would have my morning coffee, read the Qur'an, make salah, then stand in front of the train station, selling and giving dawah. This was early in the seventies. Years later, masjids popped up in the areas where we gave dawah, like on 168th Street and Hillside Ave. I also had a dawah spot in front of the bus station off of Jamaica Ave.

Then, a masjid popped up across the street from the bus station next to the library. Those people who establish those masjids are clueless of the dawah work established in those areas long before they thought about developing a masjid. After I left 168th Street, we walked to Parsons Blvd and we gave dawah at that train station.

Then we walked to Sutphin Blvd and we gave dawah at that train station. After that, it was coffee time and ta'leem. Then, we would go down the street on Sutphin Blvd across from the courthouse and give dawah at the Motor Vehicles before they moved. After that, we walked down Jamaica Ave. and gave dawah until we reached Chock Full o'Nuts. That was our headquarters.

That's where I met Mr. Neelain Muhammad, who they now call Shaykh Neelain Muhammad, who is known as the bodyguard of Muhammad Ali. If you want to know more, he can tell you about that story. During his time, my teacher and I were giving dawah in these areas of Queens by ourselves. Most of the time, I was alone because Abdullah Nafis was missing in action. Now, that's a long story.

Should University students busy themselves making electronic dawah choices like videos and DVDs?

I believe—and Allah knows best—that University students should busy themselves in learning how to give dawah. A person needs all the training he can get, so when Allah gives him his job, he will be well-equipped for it. When a person starts learning dawah, he needs to work in the trenches so he can have natural growth and development. How can you build a hundred-story building with a weak foundation? Working in the trenches helps to mold your character for dawah. It gives you the qualities of patience and tolerance. University students should work on small projects so that they will be prepared in time.

I've heard it said that "We should let others work in the field giving dawah and I should concentrate on the in-house mas-

jid teachings and university lectures because I'm on a different level—I'm scholarly."

Now, it is true that we need people to teach in the masjids and give lectures. The question I have is: was that the way our beloved Prophet ﷺ and his companions—may Allah be pleased with them—spread the message of Islam? From what has reached me, it is that they worked in the trenches with the ordinary people, they sacrificed and paid dues to establish this Deen. Many of them lost their lives. If you think you're going to spread this deen in the comfort of your masjids and the plush carpets in your Eiffel-Tower university setting with your flowery speeches, then wake up oh, sleeping giant. The only way a dream becomes a reality is that you have to wake up from your dream.

Islam has been spreading in America from the sweat of grunt Muslim soldiers of the past, alhamdulillah. For the most part, they are not even known to the masses of the Muslims. They sacrificed their lives, time, efforts, so you can lift your head in the West and proudly say you are Muslim today. Come off your pedestals and boldly go out and invite people to Islam. People need a real, living person to talk to and walk with them. If you haven't been trained, it's time to get training. Don't stop what you are doing in the service of Allah, giving classes and lectures, but don't be too embarrassed to be seen on the street with the ordinary people, helping them and inviting them to Islam.

CHAPTER 12

ABOUT THE AUTHOR

ABOUT THE AUTHOR

SHAYKH KHALID AMIN IS A Muslim African American born in New York City, who now lives in Madinah, Saudi Arabia. Shaykh Khalid has been a da'ee (caller to Islam) for over 50 years.

He began his path to Islam and became a Muslim in 1969 through an organization known as the Nation of Islam. He took his shahada in 1975 from the late Imam W.D. Muhammad, who died several years ago—may Allah forgive his sins and give him Jannah, ameen.

In 1977, Shaykh Khalid was blessed to make Hajj (pilgrimage to Makkah). Then in 1979, he was blessed to return to Makkah as a student of knowledge. He studied there for over five years in the time of the great shaykh, Shaykh Ibn Baz rahimahullah. The author has been a continuous student of Islam ever since he returned to the Hejaz (the area of Saudi Arabia where the two most holy cities in Islam are found) in 1979.

One of his closest teachers was Shaykh Muhammad Amin of Ethiopia who died and was buried in 2019 in Makkah—

may Allah have mercy on him and grant him the highest level of Jennah. Other sheikhs with whom he has studied include Sheikh of the Haram, Muhammad Subail, Sheikh Ali Al Hind, Sheikh Muhammad Tayyib AshShingiti and many others, may Allah have mercy on them. Shaykh Khalid has been living and studying in Makkah and Madinah off and on for about 40 years.

He is married to Fautimah Amin. They have three children, all boys; Harun, Abu Bakr, and Abdullah. All of them are hufadh of the Qur'an (one who has fully memorized the Qur'an). The youngest, Abdullah, is a graduate of Madinah University. Each of the three of them received extensive training in the methods mentioned in this book. AbuBakr is an engineer, and Harun is a builder. Each of them remains as active as their family responsibilities permit giving dawah.

Shaykh Khalid Amin lived in Morocco in the city of Casablanca with his three sons for six years as they were learning the Qur'an. They are proficient in the Arabic language and Islamic studies. All of them now live and teach in Michigan, USA.

The knowledge of giving dawah is something he learned while inviting people to the Nation of Islam, prior to studying in Makkah. After this time period, he applied the knowledge of giving dawah to his knowledge of the religion, Islam. Allah has brought untold numbers of people to Islam at his hands. Now this book and the associated seminars are designed to bring this knowledge to you. I pray Allah all involved benefit and please Allah by their works. Ameen.

Sheikh Khalid Amin—Translator

1951 Born,
1964 First introduced to Islam through association with a young man named Butch Camp. His brother (William

76X Griffen) was in the Nation of Islam and started a neighborhood basketball team called Afrasia. Through this team, Brother William introduced many of the young men to Islam, including Sheikh Khalid.

1965 First visited Temple #7, in the room above a Jehovah Witness hall. This was right after Malcolm X (Hajj Malik Shabazz—may Allah have mercy on him) was assassinated and the Temple #7 was burned to the ground. Minister Louis Farrakhan was speaking. Sheikh Khalid and his friends used to sneak to the temple because their parents were against them going.

1969 Joined the Nation of Islam in Brooklyn, New York under Minister Arthur 14X (who is now Imam Bashir in Atlanta, Georgia) and Lieutenant Richard 8X (who recently died as Farid Bayyah in Atlanta, Georgia—may Allah have mercy on him). Sheikh Khalid started processing under Minister George (Kamal Majeed). He was one of the youngest brothers on the Lieutenant staff under the first Lieutenant Clarence 7X (Imam Hussein Shabazz) and Captain Joseph (Yusef Shah). Captain Joseph was made captain of by Mister Elijah Muhammad and Minister Malcolm. Sheikh Khalid drove the school bus for The University of Islam for several years. He was young, single and entrusted with the children. Director Clark (Imam Muhammad Saddiq) was the principal and Lieutenant Richard 8X was in charge of transportation and Brother Andrew was in charge of the gas station. Sheikh Khalid also worked under Captain Yusef Shah several years and helped him to establish his daily juice business along with Brother Cleophus and the Captain's wife, Sister Sylvia Shah. These brothers were contemporaries of Al Hajj Malik Shabazz—may Allah have mercy on him—and they represented the foundation for Sheikh Khalid's training.

1973 Sheikh Khalid was selling 1,000 Muhammad Speaks (later the Bilalian News) Newspapers per week. He and his crew, The Couriers, took shahada under Imam Warith Deen Muhammad, may Allah have mercy on him, in 1975 after Mr. Elijah Muhammad died. He was responsible for the group of brothers called The Couriers who traveled all over, blazing the trail for Imam W. D. Muhammad's lectures. They were blessed to give numerous shahadas through this work and continued until 1979.

1977 Sheikh Khalid was awarded a free trip for Hajj. It was presented to him by Imam W. D. Muhammad personally for selling newspapers and giving dawah. The trip was sponsored by Brothers in Islam, Herbert Muhammad (Jabir Muhammad) and Muhammad Ali. Abdul Aziz, a blind brother from who was selling 500 papers per week also made Hajj with the group that year. This was the first year the Nation of Islam, then known as the World Community of Islam, made Hajj. While there, Sheikh Khalid met Doctor Abdullah Nasif who helped him complete his application and get accepted into the Language Program at Malik Abdul Aziz University which is now called Umm Al Qura University.

1979-1981 The Arabic Language Program at Malik Abdul Aziz University.

1981-1984 Studied in Masjid Al Haram and Dar al Hadith and Studied with:

- Sheikh Muhammad Amin—Arabic Grammar
- Imam of the Haram Muhammad Subail—Arabic Grammar and Fatawa
- Sheikh Saeed Sulula—Science of Hadith
- Sheikh Ali Al Hind—Sahih Bukhari
- Sheikh Muhammad AsSomali—Hadith

- Sheikh Muhammad Tayyub ash Shingiti—Muwatta Imam Malik and Alfiya Ibn Malik (Grammar)
- Sheikh Muhammad Deen—Memorization of Qur'an
- Sheikh Mekki—Tafseer of Qur'an
- Sheikh Jumaa' from—Hadith
- Sheikh Abdul Aziz Bin Baz—Tauhid, Arkan al Islam

1984 Returned to the United States and married. Sheikh Khalid spent some time teaching Arabic and Islamic Studies. He was active in giving dawah, teaching at Masjid Madinah in Saudi Arabia, establishing a tradition of hosting guests and being blessed with 3 boys. He established a Qur'an class in South Miami, Florida that continues to this day. He established Arabic and Islamic Studies classes at the Joseph Caleb Center in Liberty City, Miami, Florida, as well.

1984 Studied martial arts under Professor Moses Powell for Jujitsu and with one of his black belts, Neelain Muhammad, also for Jujitsu.

1986 Imam at Masjid Muhammad. This masjid was built from the ground up by African American Muslims, originally from the community of Imam W. D. Muhammad. In answer to a division in this Masjid, Imam Hassan, a Palestinian Imam at a neighboring masjid, requested Sheikh Khalid assume the position of Imam as a neutral party and to teach the members of Masjid Muhammad Islam.

1988 Imam of Masjid Tauba. During this period, Allah blessed him to be at the helm of establishing the following things: a person to person dawah program downtown and Islamic studies and dawah classes at The University of Michigan and Michigan State University. A Qur'an school in his home continued the tradition of taking care of guests. All of this work, alHamdulillah, was rewarded with countless shahadas. He trained people in giving dawah and doing business to support the dawah efforts so they wouldn't have to ask anyone but Allah. Under his leadership and encouragement, alHamdulillah, the Masjid Tauba community later acquired a larger facility for Masjid Tauba with an attached store that continued the tradition of a self-supporting Masjid and dawah effort, alHamdulillah.

1988 Additionally, as a result of contact with a Christian food pantry headed by a sister who later took shahada, the community has also established a food program for the needy.

1988 Studied under Sensei Khalid Shakoor from Detroit, Michigan in Aki JuJitsu and Aikido. Earned a black belt in Aiki Jiu Jitsu.

1994 Travelled to Morocco with his 3 sons where the 4 of them studied hifz of Qur'an under Faqih Abdul Kabeer Mitir. His sons all became hafiz of Qur'an, alHamdulillah; and he increased his hifz during this time and studied tafsir of Qur'an.

1994 Studied with Sensei Luqman Abdul Hakeem (a student of Umada Sensei who was a student of O Sensei, the founder of Aikido) for 5 years. Sensei Luqman was also in the Nation of Islam under Al Hajj Malik Shabazz . Through their association, Sheikh Khalid learned a great deal about American history, the contributions and the effects it has had on its citizens of African decent.

2000 Returned to Ann Arbor, Michigan where he re-established a Qur'an school. The teachers were his three sons, Harun, AbuBakr and Abdullah for memorization of Qur'an; Harun is still teaching memorization of Qur'an at Masjid Tauba. Sheikh Khalid taught Arabic language, Islamic Law (Fiqh), Aqidah Tahawiyyah, Al Ajromea (Arabic Grammar), the Madinah Language Program (Conversational Arabic), Balug al Maram (Hadith), and Tafsir of Qur'an, all exclusively in the Arabic language.

2001 Met with Sheikh Muhammad Amin in Makkah, Saudi Arabia, as he does every year, to visit with him and offer him whatever services he can. At that time, he was given the honor and permission to translate all 32 volumes of his Tafsir of Qur'an, The Generous Food of Hospitality in the Courtyard of the Gardens of Rest and Provision from its original Arabic to English. Sheikh Muhammad also presented him with a first edition, fresh from the printer.

2002 Made Hijrah to Madinah, Saudi Arabia with his family. Two of his sons are here studying on the hands of the 'ulema. He's translating the Tafsir of his beloved teacher in Islam, Sheikh Muhammad Amin al Harari from Makkah al Mukarama. His boys are continuing their studies in Qur'an, Islamic Studies and Martial Arts. Sheikh Khalid is presently studying with the following Sheikhs of Madinah to continue his education and for continuous improvement of his translation skills:

- Sheikh Ahmar Walid Hubbullah, may Allah have mercy on him—Fiqh al Imam Malik
- Sheikh Muhammad al Aghatha, may Allah have mercy on him—Tafsir al Qur'an
- Sheikh Abdul Muhsin Hamad al Ibad al Badar—40 Hadith
- Sheikh Muhammad Mahmoud al Imam, may Allah have mercy on him—Tafsir al Qur'an

- Sheikh Muhammad Ali Athani, may Allah have mercy on him—Bulugh al Maram, Hadith, Fiqh, Shari'a
- Sheikh Hamed Akram—Aqeedah

2006-2021 Studied with Sensei AbdurRahman Ogues, Godan (5th Dan) Awarded Yandan (4th Dan)

Author: welovequran@gmail.com

Ambassadors of Humanity Presents: QR Codes to Enhance Your Reading Experience

At Ambassadors of Humanity, our main goal is to give people the opportunity to understand Islam as it has always been, whether brought by Adam, Abraham, Moses, Jesus or Muhammad (May Allah's prayers and blessings be upon them all). We would love to hear from you whether your interest in Islam is scholarly, curiosity, or a passion for spreading the truth.

Below we have provided QR codes for your convenience in contacting us and enhancing your reading and learning further through our various social media channels and networks.

Welcome.

Account	Purpose & Benefits	QR Code
Ambassadors of Humanity Official YouTube Channel	Videos/Podcasts/ Seminars	
Ambassadors of Humanity Website	Book Purchase: Individual and Discounted Bulk	

Amazon Da'wah: The Lost Call of Islam	Book Purchase	
Ambassadors of Humanity Whatsapp Channel	Customer Service: All inquiries and requests can be directed to this channel.	
Ambassadors of Humanity Official Instagram Account	See where we are going and what we are doing	
Ambassadors of Humanity Official Twitter Page	Info Feed/Comments	
Ambassadors of Humanity Official TikTok Account	Info Feed	

Ambassadors of Humanity Official Telegram Channel	Info Feed/Classes	
Ambassadors of Humanity Official Facebook Account	Info Feed	

www.ingramcontent.com/pod-product-compliance
Lightning Source LLC
Chambersburg PA
CBHW052042280426
43661CB00084B/18